T0362895

# A REAL GIRL'S
# GUIDE TO
# MONEY

*by* **EFFIE ZAHOS**

*First edition originally published in 2019 by Are Media Books.*
*This edition published in 2023. Are Media Books is a division of Are Media Pty Ltd.*

**ARE MEDIA**

*Chief executive officer* Jane Huxley

*Group publisher* Nicole Byers

*Books director* David Scotto

*Author* Effie Zahos

*Editor* Maria Bekiaris

*Researcher* Nicola Field

*Sub editors* Bob Christensen, Debbie Duncan

*Managing editor* Stephanie Kistner

*Senior designer* Jeannel Cunanan

*Cover photographer* Yianni Aspradakis

*Cover stylist* Rosie Mckay

*Cover hair & makeup artist*
Stella Anogianakis

Printed in China
by 1010 Printing International

A catalogue record for this book is available
from the National Library of Australia.

ISBN 978-1-76122-121-7

© Are Media Pty Limited 2023

ABN 18 053 273 546

This publication is copyright.
No part of it may be reproduced or
transmitted in any form without
the written permission of the publisher.

Published by Are Media Books,
a division of Are Media Pty Ltd,
54 Park St, Sydney; GPO Box 4088,
Sydney, NSW 2001, Australia
Ph +61 2 9282 8000
www.aremedia.com.au

**ORDER BOOKS**
phone 136 116 (within Australia)
or order online at
*www.aremediabooks.com.au*

**DISCLAIMER**

Let's get real … while I hope this book helps you on your path to financial success I'd hate for you
to solely rely on it. It was never written as a substitute for, nor was it intended to replace or
supersede, independent or other professional advice.

I am not a financial adviser so the information in this book is intended as general guidance only.
Great information, though, and there's plenty to be said about being financially savvy.

Given that the circumstances and investment objectives of individual users have not been taken
into account in the preparation of material in this book, please be sure to make your own inquiries
before making any investment decisions.

This edition includes information current at the time of writing.

# Dedication

*This book is dedicated to the strongest woman I know, my mother Angela. Growing up in a remote little Greek village as the youngest of 12 children, she wasn't given the gift of financial literacy – had she been given that privilege, she would have soared even further!*

# Contents

# A REAL GIRL'S
# GUIDE TO
# MONEY

*A lot has happened since the first edition of this book was released in early
2019 – we've survived a pandemic, a recession, seen the first rate hikes in
years, and the cost of living is through the roof. There have also been changes to
superannuation – the $450 Super Guarantee (SG) threshold was removed and
the SG rate was increased – and there's also more help for first home buyers.*

But, despite all the changes over the past four years, when it comes to our
personal finances the fundamental principles remain the same. So while, of
course, I have made all the necessary updates to reflect what has changed, the
key themes and messages in that first edition still stand today.

As I was writing this book originally, I kept thinking about the conversations
my girlfriends and I have about money. They often challenge me about what I
do or don't do with my money – and I don't mind that at all. I like the fact that
we talk about money and after a couple of wines, nothing is off limits. Surely
we can't be the only group of girls who wonder, "How can she afford that?"

If it's not a chat with your girlfriends, maybe it's a chat with yourself.
Sometimes that little voice in your head knows exactly what to ask. "You earn

$150,000 a year, why are you still broke?" Or maybe you're hoping to get on the property ladder but that voice keeps telling you "I'll never own a home."

My greatest fear (which many people now know) is retiring in a polyester outfit and drinking cask wine because I haven't saved enough to live the lifestyle I'm accustomed to. This may sound superficial but, jokes aside, the lack of money women have in retirement is a big issue.

*This book was – and still is – for every woman who has that voice in her head or a group of friends who want answers.*

I tackle each stage in life, from getting your first job and falling in (and out) of love and starting a family to planning for those golden years.

Each chapter tackles a real question and offers a solution, covering topics such as a three-bucket approach to help you budget and save, the five triggers that cause you to spend and the fixes, as well as the $1+2+3$ = retirement plan. If you're time-poor you'll find an "If you only do one thing" tip in each chapter with easy suggestions to follow to help you on the road to wealth.

And with inflation hitting a 21-year high in 2022, I felt it was important to include something in this edition specifically to help beat the cost of living. That's why I added a bonus Bill Buster Action Plan with plenty of tips and tricks to cut the costs of the everyday bills that seem to be taking a larger chunk out of our budgets.

The Money Makeover – which puts the fun back into saving – has also made a comeback. It includes 26 challenges to complete that will help you make money, save money or simply get your financial affairs in order. I want you to think of it like a big game of bingo. It's simple really – you pick any task from the list, action it, record any savings, cross it off and move on to the next one.

There's no specific order and no time constraints. If you feel like doing one a week go for it, if you want to skip a week it's not a problem and if you want to do three in a week I'm all for it. Do it at the pace that works for you.

The Bill Buster Action Plan and Money Makeover go hand in hand to help you take greater control of your finances – something that is more important than ever given the world we are living in.

I just want to make sure we keep things real. I don't pretend to be a financial guru, nor am I a financial adviser, but after 25 years working in the personal finance space I've picked up some real money gems. Interestingly, the ones that have stuck with me are the simple ones, like it's not what you earn that counts, it's what you spend; compounding interest can make you a millionaire, and pay yourself first.

It's easy to take risks and look good when the market is up but it's far more inspirational if you can build financial security in an everyday situation because, let's face it, most of us sit in this world.

The information in this book is straightforward and easy to understand – exactly what I'm known for and what I've been doing in print, TV and radio for over two decades. If you are looking for a kickstart – something to help you control your finances rather than them controlling you – then this book is it.

# If you only do one thing...

Make the time to focus on your finances. Promise yourself you will review your household bills with the help of the Bill Buster Action Plan and give the Money Makeover bingo challenge a go.

## LET'S GET REAL ...

In my late 30s I was invited to a party at another parent's house. My husband and I were greeted at the door with Veuve and hors d'oeuvres ... life couldn't look any better than this! Our hosts had it all: designer threads, children at private school, a McMansion and a couple of Beemers in the driveway. How did she (or in this case "they") afford that? A couple of flutes later my conversation with them jumped from small chat to big talk. These people weren't poor but they were broke, living well beyond their means.

It's not unusual for people to divulge their money secrets to me. I guess it's no different to me cornering a physio at a party and talking to them about my sore back. Was I of any help? I'm not too sure but I do know that sometime later they took control of their situation by downsizing their home and pulling their children out of private school.

If you've ever asked yourself "How can she afford that?", know that all is not what it may appear to be. She either sticks to a budget and has her eye on the prize or she lives beyond her means.

# CHAPTER

# 1

## How can she afford that?

# Fast fact

*If you saved from the age of 25 to 35 and then stopped, you would still have more than someone who started at 35 and saved until they were 65. It's a simple but powerful calculation from a JP Morgan retirement guide that highlights the magic of compound interest.*

## NOBODY REALLY TEACHES YOU HOW TO MANAGE A BUDGET. IT'S EXPECTED THAT YOU JUST KNOW HOW TO DO IT. AFTER ALL, IT'S EASY – RIGHT?

You just fill in a budget planner, track your expenses and voilà! Whatever money is left over you save. If only it were that easy. The fact is that many of us rely on credit cards, buy now pay later and pay advance services, so I'm guessing there are a few of us who could do with budgeting 101.

Funnily enough, I know plenty of people who don't have a budget. They're quite happy to spend money on piccolos and shoes as long as they're reaching their saving goals. And that can be fine. As long as you've set some goals, you know how much you need to save and you're putting it away, does it matter where the rest of your money is going?

Well, yes and no. Unless you're flush with cash (and I mean you're earning some serious coin), there is some real benefit to understanding where your money is going.

Find out where it is going and you'll uncover your spending habits. Uncover your spending habits and you'll be able to work out why you do what you do. Work this out and you can then break those old habits and unleash the saver in you. Do this and you'll have the perfect budget!

When it comes to saving, our brain isn't always our best friend. Economists and psychologists have long recognised the behavioural issues that can hold us back from saving. If you're earning a good income and don't understand why you're still broke, then it's your habits that you should focus on. You can read more about this in Chapter 14 ("I earn $150k, why am I still broke?").

If all this talk about doing a budget has you hyperventilating, then don't fret because there are ways to set a budget without having to over-scrutinise every cent you spend.

# FIRST, SET YOUR FORMULA

*There's no shortage of budget formulas to help you reach your goals, including paying your bills on time and being able to take those much-needed holidays. A popular option is the 70:20:10 plan. Here's how it works.*

## Divide your money between:

- 70% for everyday living costs (rent or home loan, transport, clothing, food and utilities).
- 20% for saving.
- 10% for splurging.

The formula that works for you can vary but the non-negotiable part is always to allocate a percentage of your take-home pay to savings.

### Next, set up some buckets

Instead of lumping your "everyday living" expenses into a single bucket, for instance, open multiple buckets (accounts) and give each of them a nickname. You might have one account for school fees, another for household bills and so on.

The same goes for savings. The 20% can be further broken down between savings buckets – 5% can go to your rainy day bucket, 10% to your holiday bucket and 5% to the "get ahead" bucket.

Using buckets within buckets makes it easier to achieve multiple goals. You can allocate a set sum to each bucket, track your progress and fine-tune your budget for each target.

Choose fee-free online savings accounts with a healthy ongoing rate rather than a short-lived introductory rate, and you can't lose.

# Not sure of the formula?

If you're not too sure whether you should allocate 70% of your income to everyday living costs, or 60%, then the easiest way to work out what's best for you is to delve a little deeper into your finances by asking these three questions:

## 1. WHERE DOES YOUR MONEY GO?

This is where you'll need to fill in a budget. Essentially, you list what you spend and you take that away from the amount you earn. This might be a matter of putting pen to paper, entering your data into an Excel spreadsheet or using a budgeting app. It doesn't matter which one you use – it's just important that you work it out. Hopefully, after working on your budget, you'll find you've earned more than you've spent. If not, or you'd like to save even more, then move to the next step.

## 2. CAN YOU CUT COSTS?

Chances are there are a handful of regular bills that are wolfing down your pay packet. This is where you need to take a good look at whether or not you can get a better deal, or maybe give a particular service the flick altogether. There are so many simple steps you can take to reduce your expenses – and, yes, taking your lunch to work might be one of them but it won't be your only option. You'll find more ideas later in this chapter and in the Bill Buster Action Plan starting on page 202.

## 3. CAN YOU EARN MORE?

Don't neglect the other side of the ledger – your income. When it comes to making extra cash, the sharing economy offers plenty of opportunities. Whether you decide to rent out your spare room, share your car or pet-sit, you can boost the money coming in.

# Work out where your money is going

These days working out where your money is going can be much easier than filling in a spreadsheet. There are a number of fantastic (and often free) apps that can help you track your spending as well as any money coming in.

### *Check the apps offered by your bank or take a look at these options:*

## 1. FROLLO

*Cost: Free.* With Frollo you can link all of your financial accounts (transaction, savings, credit card, loans, super, investment and more) to see them all in one place. You can see where your money is going as Frollo automatically organises your transactions into categories.

## 2. GOODBUDGET

*Cost: Free for the basic version or $US8pm/$US70pa for a version with more options.* This app is based on the envelope budgeting system. The idea is that your expenses are divided into virtual envelopes for various budget categories. You then take out money out of the designated envelope to spend. That way you can keep track of your spending and make sure you don't go over your budget for that category.

## 3. SPENDEE

*Cost: Free for the basic version, $US14.99pa for Plus and $US22.99pa for Premium.* Spendee helps you keep track of your cash flow and lets you set budgets for categories so you can stop yourself from overspending. The drawback is that you can only sync account details for a small number of Australian financial institutions so you may have to manually enter expenses.

Hopefully, once you've completed the budget there'll be some money left over – meaning that you spend less than you earn. If not, then there's a bit of a problem, so you'll need to identify areas where you can cut back.

# If you only do one thing...

Pay yourself $15 every time you take your lunch to work. Set up an online saver and call it "EAT ME!" Transfer $15 into this account just before you take a bite. If you've forgotten to take your lunch to work, do not use this money to pay for it. Assuming you're 25 and take your lunch twice a week, you'll have $67,024 by the time you hit 50, assuming a return of 4% a year. Now that's some serious lunch money!

# *Easy ways* TO CUT YOUR COSTS

*If you're spending more than you earn, then it's a matter of looking at your big expenses and identifying how you can trim them. There's the mortgage or rent, gas and electricity, the groceries, phone and internet, petrol … the list goes on and on.*

While all these expenses may be necessary, this doesn't mean you can't work towards making the bills smaller each month.

First up, always make sure you have the right product. For example, shop around and compare the various offers from gas and electricity providers before signing up. The same goes for phone service providers – check out the deals on offer and choose the one that best suits your needs. Think about how you use your phone and what's right for you.

And if you're not on the best deal, then don't be afraid to switch – the potential savings can be huge. For example, let's say you're paying 4.5% on your mortgage but can refinance to a loan charging just 3.65%. On a mortgage of $400,000 over 25 years you'd save around $2256 in the next year alone and be ahead by more than $56,000 over the life of the loan.

Refinancing can come with costs. So check the rate you're currently paying, ask your lender if they can offer a better deal and, if not, do the sums to see if taking your business elsewhere will deliver real savings.

Before you give your bank the flick, be sure to calculate your break-even point to make sure it's worth the move. Add up the costs to refinance and divide them by your monthly savings. For example, if it costs $1000 to switch but you'd save $50 a month in repayments, it would take 20 months to "break even". You had better hope in that case that your new lender will remain competitive long enough for you to recoup your costs!

You can use the "mortgage switching" calculator on moneysmart.gov.au to work out how much you'll save and how long it will take to recover the costs.

*Here are a few more ways to slash your expenses:*

### • DELETE AT LEAST ONE APP FROM YOUR PHONE

Uber, Uber Eats, Deliveroo, Afterpay, Zip Pay or Tipple ... they're all very
handy but this sort of convenience makes it easy to spend – and overspend.
I don't know about you but for some reason I justified my Uber trips by saying
they were cheaper than a taxi. Trouble is, I was taking so many Uber rides that
I was on the verge of having a personal driver. Whatever your app of choice,
grab a copy of your purchase history (it's all online) and if you're shocked
about how much you're spending, then delete that app from your smartphone.

### • SET UP YOUR OWN "BUY NOW, PAY LATER" ACCOUNT

Digital disrupters are changing the way we pay, and while some like Afterpay
and Zip Pay don't charge any interest (only late fees), they do make shopping
far more tempting. Technically, you could take home a $200 pair of jeans with
as little as $50 upfront. Instead, set up your own account. Put, say, $1000 in it
and only use this account to shop. Pay yourself back in four equal instalments
rather than signing up with an outside party. Chances are when you've saved up
the cash and you're staring at it you may be more reluctant to part with it.
Either way, you are in control.

### • FOLLOW A 5:2 MONEY DIET

You've heard of the 5:2 intermittent fasting diets. You eat normally on five
days of the week and restrict your intake to 500-600 calories on each of the
other two days. Well, the 5:2 money diet is similar but it works the other way
around – you fast for five days and only spend on two. Author Kate Harrison
applied this advice in her book, *5:2 Your Life*. You can apply the 5:2 concept
literally or figuratively. I like to use it loosely as I do with most of my diets.
Try not to make any discretionary spending Monday to Friday – no coffees,
no bottled water, no takeaways and so on – and on the weekends resume
spending as normal.

## • DON'T HIDE BEHIND CPW

The "cost per wear" formula is an easy answer to "Should I buy it?" But let's not kid ourselves here. Yes, most fashionistas would agree that Louboutins at just $2.64 per day are a bargain but what true fashionista wears the same pair of shoes for 365 days. Nobody does. There's the trap. CPW is a false economy. Open your wardrobe and take a good look at how many pairs of shoes or skirts or tops you have. Do we really need all this stuff? Stick to high-quality pieces and work the wardrobe you already own. It may even be worth paying a stylist to come in and help. It could be money well spent if it stops you from splurging.

## • TAKE BACK ONE "OUTSOURCE"

If you're outsourcing your ironing, cleaning, cooking, gardening and whatever else you don't have time for, make sure that your hourly rate is at least double the cost of the outsourcing. If not, rein it back in! You may even find that some activities such as gardening can be a great way to reconnect with your family (and let's not forget the incidental exercise!).

## • ASK FOR A DISCOUNT

If you're spending a bit on dry cleaning or grooming, for example, put a case together and present it to your provider as to why they should give you a discount. Put your business out for tender. Believe me, if you're a regular customer, they don't want to lose you. By showing them how much business you give them, a discount of 5%-10%, for instance, is a no-brainer for them to keep you.

## • USE THE 48-HOUR RULE

The 48-hour rule is one I often use when I'm tempted to splurge on something – I sleep on it for two days and if I still really want it, then I will go back and buy it. I also use the time to think about other options – can I borrow something similar or buy it second-hand?

## • REDUCE WASTE

Food waste costs Australian households between $2000 and $2500 each year – that's at least $38 a week! Skip the waste by getting creative. Make it your challenge to use every piece of fruit, vegetable or meat in your fridge. There's a reason why we have pizza night on Fridays – it's to clear out all the deli meat and cheeses that didn't get used up in the school lunches.

# Need to know

Work out your debt load. Divide your total debts (this includes your rent or mortgage, minimum credit card repayments and personal loans) by your total net income and then convert that decimal to a percentage. Let's say, for example, your monthly household income is $6500 and the monthly payments on your debt load totals $3000. Divide $3000 by $6500 and you get 0.46 (or 46%). How much is too much? You'll know if your debt load is too high but ideally you want to stay south of 40%.

# *Smart ways* TO EARN MORE

*One way to fatten up your cash flow is to look for opportunities in the sharing economy. Here are a few options:*

## • TURN SPARE SPACE INTO SPARE CASH

Open up a room in your home for short-term accommodation. According to the Airbnb calculator, renting out a single bedroom in Sydney could add an extra $1851 each month to your bank balance. Or rent out an unused garage or car space through Parkhound and pocket up to $450 a month.

## • JOIN A RIDE-SHARING SERVICE

Put your car to work by signing up as an Uber driver, or rent out your car for others to drive through the likes of DriveMyCar. On a car worth $24,000 you could earn an extra $840 a month.

## • FLEX SOME MUSCLE

Run some errands, shift some furniture or do a delivery – and earn up to $5000 each month doing odd jobs with Airtasker.

## • TURN THAT JUNK OF YOURS INTO CASH

Go through your home to find items you no longer use or want. It might be books, homewares, toys or even clothes. Aussies stand to make about $7000 per household from their unwanted items, according to a 2022 report by Gumtree. List unwanted items for sale on sites like Gumtree or eBay, or consider Etsy for vintage goodies or collectables. Designer brands are generally in big demand, so if you have a Louis Vuitton handbag or Gucci sunnies you are happy to part with then you could make a decent sum.

Consignment stores can also be a good way to offload designer clothing and high-end apparel. It pays to shop around because the commission charged by different outlets can be as high as 50% of the sale price.

# Checklist

☐ *Set up your budget formula and savings buckets.*

☐ *Do a budget and work out what percentage of your income is going where (living costs, savings, splurging).*

☐ *Look for ways to slash your bills.*

☐ *Boost your savings potential by earning extra cash.*

☐ *Remember to declare any income earned in the sharing economy.*

## LET'S GET REAL ...

The best thing I ever did was learn to pay myself first, set up money buckets and automate my savings. Now, while I may sound perfect, I was far from it. Something happened in my 30s that I'm not too proud of. I went on a spending binge and it was funded by pay rises. Let me explain. Getting a pay rise can have the same effect as several cosmo cocktails. You're excited and only too happy to live the dream with family and friends. Some of the carnage of my 30s can be still found in my closet. Good news, though. Reality kicked back in and I curbed my spending by upping my savings. Later I even overcompensated for the guilt by setting up periodical payments of just $40 each payday to go into my kids' accounts. I almost didn't do it, as I thought $40 was too little. The money was never an investment for them (that I set up when they were born) but a cash pot to be used either for their first car or to help out with a post-HSC holiday, which for my eldest came around faster than I would have ever thought possible. (And in case you're wondering, she did use the money for a trip to Japan.) The lesson here is to never underestimate small change.

# CHAPTER

2

How much should
I be saving?

# Fast fact

**A 25-year-old making $800 a week (after tax) would need to save only 10% of their pay and they'd have over $596,113 at 67. This assumes a return of 5%pa and that they never get a pay rise.**

## HOW MUCH SHOULD YOU SAVE? THE SIMPLE ANSWER TO THIS IS AS MUCH AS YOU CAN. BUT THIS WOULD BE A VERY SHORT CHAPTER IF I LEFT THINGS THERE!

The truth is there are no hard and fast rules about how much you should put away each week or month. It really depends on your goals, how long you have to reach them and the risk you're willing to take. That said, I do think that aiming to save at least 10% of your pay (regardless of how much you earn) is a great place to begin. It's better to start small and actually save rather than set yourself a ridiculous target and fail.

You can then build up the amount slowly over time. Let's say you are paid $800 a week and save 10% – that would be $80 a week. After six months or so increase that to 12% and you'd only have to put an extra $16 away each week.

At the end of the day, though, what is most important is that you are putting away money on a regular basis and that it's not just an afterthought. In Chapter 1, I spoke about setting up "buckets" and one of those should be for savings. If you have worked on your budget you will have a better idea of how much you can afford to save. The key is to arrange for that amount to be automatically transferred to a separate account before you get your hands on it.

To be a successful saver I think having a goal – or two – can really help. Saving for a rainy day is great but it doesn't motivate the same way as a trip to New York with the girls would. You're more likely to spend less and put aside money if you have something tangible in mind.

You might have more than one thing on your list, so think about breaking up goals into short-term, medium-term and long-term. For example, in the short term you may want those Louboutins, in the medium term a trip to Positano and in the long term a house deposit or your kids' education expenses.

If you're saving for multiple goals, instead of lumping your savings into a single account, set up more buckets. So if you're saving 20% from each pay, that can be further broken down between savings buckets: 5% can go to your shoes bucket; 5% to your holiday bucket; and 10% to the house deposit bucket.

You can open separate accounts, each dedicated to a particular goal. Give each savings account a nickname that represents what you're saving for. Most banks will let you do this online. For your longer-term goals – say, four or five years ahead – you should consider investing rather than a savings account. Chapter 7 ("I'm ready to start investing") has more tips on that.

# HAVE A PLAN

Think about exactly how much money you'll need and how long you have to save it. The savings goals calculator at moneysmart.gov.au comes in handy here because it can help you work out how much you need to save regularly to reach your goal in a specified time frame. For example, if you want to save $5000 in two years, you'll need to put aside $202 each month to reach your goal, assuming an interest rate of 3%. If you want $20,000 in five years, it's $301 each month, assuming 4% interest. Check out the table below to get an idea of how much you need to put away each month to reach certain amounts.

## What you need to put away each month

| | INVESTMENT PERIOD AND RATE OF RETURN | | |
|---|---|---|---|
| | 2 years (3%) | 5 years (4%) | 7 years (5%) |
| $2000 | $81 | $30 | $20 |
| $5000 | $202 | $75 | $50 |
| $7500 | $303 | $113 | $74 |
| $10,000 | $404 | $150 | $99 |
| $15,000 | $606 | $226 | $149 |
| $20,000 | $808 | $301 | $199 |
| $25,000 | | $376 | $248 |
| $30,000 | | $451 | $298 |
| $35,000 | | $526 | $347 |
| $40,000 | | $601 | $397 |
| $45,000 | | $676 | $447 |
| $50,000 | | $752 | $496 |
| $60,000 | | | $596 |
| $70,000 | | | $695 |
| $80,000 | | | $794 |
| $90,000 | | | $893 |
| $100,000 | | | $993 |

*Source: Moneysmart.gov.au savings calculator*

Always be on the lookout for ways to give your savings a boost – any time you receive a larger sum of money, through a tax refund for example, put that straight into your savings.

The same goes for a pay rise. Even if it's just an extra $10 a week, arrange to have that transferred straight to savings. You won't miss what you never had!

If you pay off a personal loan or credit card, keep up the repayments but make them to yourself. Deposit the amount that used to go towards repaying the debt straight into your savings account.

## Staying on track

Sometimes we all need a bit of a nudge in the right direction. Consider enlisting the help of a friend. Let's call them your "savings buddy". Ideally, it would be someone who is also trying to save. Check in with them each week and if you are tempted to dip into your savings for a new handbag, call them to talk you out of it.

*There are a few apps that can help, too. Check out these three:*

### 1. LOOT: SAVINGS MONEY TRACKER

*Cost: Free.* Only available on iOS. It describes itself as a "3D money jar". Set your savings goal and each time you add money you will see the money jar filling up. It's a great way to visualise your progress.

### 2. HABITBULL HABIT TRACKER

*Cost: Free.* I think saving should really be a habit, which is why I like this app. You set up a "habit" (or multiple habits) – it can be anything you like, for example to save money each week. You tell HabitBull how you went and it keeps track for you. There are graphs to show you how long you keep the streak alive.

### 3. QUITZILLA

*Cost: Free.* Are your bad habits costing you money? Give up one vice and add the money you would have spent to your savings. So instead of buying two $20 bottles of wine each week, buy just one and then put the $20 into savings. This app will let you see how much you've saved since you ditched your bad habit. Seeing the savings you've made could help motivate you to continue. You can add as many things as you like to your list of items to quit and watch the savings add up.

# _Saving_ CAN BE FUN

_Saving money is not all about sacrificing everything you love. There are some pain-free – and dare I say fun – challenges to give you a kick-start._

## 1. 52-WEEK CHALLENGE

This is one I have used with my kids. It's a popular one to start at the beginning of the year but there's no need to wait for a new year. The idea is you save $1 in week one and increase it by $1 each week – so $5 in week five, $20 in week 20 and so on. At the end of week 52 you'll have stashed away $1378. You can also put a spin on this and do it in reverse – that is, put away $52 in week one and reduce it by $1 as the weeks go by.

## 2. THE ENVELOPE CHALLENGE

This involves getting 100 envelopes and labelling them from 1 to 100. You then shuffle them up and each day pull one out at random. Whatever number is written on the envelope is what you have to save that day. You can add the cash to the envelope or transfer money to an online account. At the end of 100 days you'll have saved $5050. If this seems too much then you can start with fewer envelopes or do it every second day instead of every day.

## 3. COKE BOTTLE CHALLENGE

Each time you get a $2 coin you pop it in a Coke (or any soft drink) bottle. Apparently, a 600ml bottle will hold about $880 when full, while a 1.25-litre bottle is meant to hold about $1900. I don't drink Coke, though, and apparently this doesn't work with a wine bottle! Admittedly, I have found this one harder to do since the pandemic as I don't use cash as often.

## 4. ROLL THE DICE CHALLENGE

You roll a six-sided dice each day and then save whatever number it lands on. If you roll a three, you have to pop $3 into your savings. You can mix this one up. You might roll two die each day or you might prefer to do it weekly. Or you can add a 0 to whatever number you roll. So rolling a three means saving $30.

## 5. WEATHER WEDNESDAY CHALLENGE

Each Wednesday you find the highest temperature in your city or state and then save that amount. So, when the mercury hits 40 degrees, you add $40 into your savings. You can opt for the lowest temperature if that's easier.

# If you only do one thing...

Pay yourself first. Set up regular automatic direct debits from your everyday account into your savings. Time the transfers to coincide with paydays to avoid overdrawing your transaction account.

# Need to know

*It doesn't make sense to put money in the bank earning 2% interest if you need to pay a debt charging 18%! Focus on paying off "bad" debts such as credit cards before you really get stuck into saving.*

# *The best place to* STASH YOUR CASH

*So you've made the commitment to put money away each pay; the next question is where you should put it.*

If you have a mortgage, then it's a good idea to stash any savings in your offset account or a redraw facility. If not, here are some of your options:

## ONLINE SAVINGS ACCOUNTS

These accounts usually pay a fairly high rate, have no minimum balance requirements and charge low or no fees. To deposit or withdraw money you need to transact online. Often they have introductory promotional rates available to new customers for a limited period. Be sure to find out what the rate will be after the promo period is over. You may consider moving your savings to take advantage of a promo offer with a different provider after it ends.

There are also "bonus saver" versions that pay you "bonus" interest if you meet certain conditions – for example, you make at least one deposit and no withdrawals in a particular month. If you don't meet these requirements you'll get the standard rate, which is usually next to nothing. Some are more flexible than others. For example, you may be able to make one withdrawal a month. It's important to understand the rules for earning the bonus interest.

## TERM DEPOSITS

With a term deposit you lock away your money for a set period – between one month and five years – and you'll be paid a fixed amount of interest. Generally the more money you lock away, and the longer the period, the higher the interest. These are ideal for people tempted to spend their money because there is usually a penalty fee if you want to take out your money before the term is up. Also be sure to check the rate before it rolls over as you may be able to get a better rate elsewhere.

## NOTICE SAVER ACCOUNTS

These are similar to term deposits but instead of locking away your money for a set period, the catch is that you have to give the institution a certain period of notice that you want to access your money. The minimum notice period is usually 31 days but 60-day and 90-day options are also available. Unlike with a term deposit, you can top up your savings.

## THE KEY TO CHOOSING THE BEST OPTION FOR YOU IS TO THINK ABOUT HOW YOU'LL USE THE ACCOUNT.

If you don't think you'll be accessing your money regularly, go for the one that pays the highest rate of interest. If you think you'll need to withdraw money at very short notice, then you may need to sacrifice some interest and opt for an account with more flexibility.

Also think about what type of saver or spender you are. If you're likely to spend your savings when you spot something you like, perhaps an account with limited access is more likely to help you reach your goals.

Comparison sites are a great place to shop around for the best-paying account. Here are a few things to think about when shopping for a savings account:

• *What is the interest rate?* Ask when interest is calculated and how often it is paid. If there is an introductory rate find out what it will revert to once the promotional period is over.

• *What fees will you have to pay?*

• *Do you have the option of ATM or branch access or can you only transact online?*

• *Are there any rules you need to know about?* For example, do you need to deposit a certain amount each month into a particular account or will you be penalised for withdrawals?

Something to remember, though, is that nobody got rich from putting money in a savings account. Saving is not the same as investing. If you have reached your savings goal and still have some savings left as an emergency fund, then consider taking the leap into the world of investing. Check out Chapter 7 ("I'm ready to start investing") if you're ready to take that next step.

# Checklist

☐ *Aim to save at least 10% of your take-home pay.*

☐ *Define your goals – short, medium and long term.*

☐ *Set up your savings buckets to achieve your goals.*

☐ *Get some help if you need it – find apps or even a savings buddy to keep you accountable.*

☐ *Take part in fun challenges to kick-start your savings.*

☐ *Have a plan to help you reach your target but don't be scared to modify it as your life changes.*

☐ *Find the right place to stash your cash.*

☐ *It is not the end of the world if you occasionally stray but make sure you learn from these experiences.*

## LET'S GET REAL ...

I'll never forget one job interview I had where the interviewer felt the need to give me his best financial tip. Okay, it was Paul Clitheroe, one of Australia's most respected financial gurus and host of Channel 9's *Money* show, where I wanted to work, so I guess it made sense for him to give me a tip or two. I remember he said something along the lines of this being the best money tip I would ever get: "Effie, it's not what you earn that counts but what you spend." It was as if the lights suddenly turned on. I got it!

It's funny that out of all the money tips he chose to give this particular one, as he offered me a job to move from banking to television but on virtually half my wage. Did I regret it? Well, given that my first assignment was to hold a butterfly frame to reflect the sun off him while we were sailing around the Whitsundays filming a story appropriately titled "Retire Rich" – yes, I did question what the hell I was doing! Fast-forward 25-odd years and it was certainly the best move I ever made. Risks in careers can certainly pay off. It's just a case of whether you can afford to take them. In my mid-20s I had no commitments so there was very little to lose.

CHAPTER

3

Got the job
- now what?

# Need to know

*Don't be afraid to get advice from the professionals if you need it. Hire a good financial adviser or wealth coach, accountant or property expert. Few people have the knowledge to handle money matters, so spend a little to acquire some.*

## CONGRATULATIONS! YOU'VE SCORED YOUR FIRST "REAL" JOB AND YOU WILL HAVE (HOPEFULLY) A DECENT AMOUNT OF MONEY HITTING YOUR BANK ACCOUNT ON A REGULAR BASIS.

Tempting as it may be to splurge on a few new outfits and nights out on the town, make sure you don't blow these early years. Trust me – when you're young you can afford to live tight. It's when you're my age that it's much harder. In the beginning, you won't mind saving on rent by living in a shared house with five others and going on backpacking holidays. In fact, all of this is fun when you're in your 20s but by the time you hit 40 forget it! So my tip is to save hard when you're young and you can relax later.

## HERE ARE THE STEPS YOU SHOULD TAKE TO SET YOURSELF UP

### Take stock of your debt

I'm hoping you can say you have a clean slate and there's no lingering credit card debt. But if I'm wrong your first step should be to focus on paying it off as fast as you can. Make repaying your loans a priority – even over your savings.

First work out exactly how bad things are. If you have only one credit card, it's pretty simple but if you have several you need to make a list and add up the total owing.

If you have multiple debts, you should focus on paying them off one at a time. Either rank your debts in order of interest rate from highest to lowest or by balance from smallest to largest. The idea is to focus on the debt at the top of the list first and pay off as much of it as you can. You should continue making the minimum repayments on any debts lower on the list. Once you have paid off the first debt you divert the extra money to the next one on the list, and so on.

If you have several debts that really add up, consolidation might be an option. This involves rolling over all your debts into a single loan. The best thing about consolidating your debt into a personal loan is that you make one repayment each month instead of several. Plus you know that at the end of the loan term the debt will be repaid and out of your hair forever.

And make sure you stay debt free. Repeat after me: "I will not buy things I don't need with money I don't have." If you have saved the money and want to go to Byron Bay for the weekend or upgrade to the latest iPhone, great! Just don't rack up a credit card debt to do it. If you do have a credit card, keep the limit low so the potential to do any real damage is minimised.

## What about student debt?

If you have a HECS-HELP debt from your student days, that's a different story. You're not charged interest but the amount is indexed annually to reflect inflation. Historically, that has been quite low, making HECS-HELP one of the cheapest debts around. We are in a period of high inflation, though, so the indexation rate jumped to 3.9% in 2022 from 0.6% the year before.

You don't have to start paying off your debt until your income reaches a certain threshold, which changes each year. You can, however, make voluntary repayments at any time and for any amount. If you are toying with the idea of making extra repayments consider the following:

• If you have any high-interest debt then you may be better off focusing on clearing that first.

• Can you get a better return on your money elsewhere? If yes, that might be a better option than paying off your HECS-HELP debt.

• Are there any other financial goals – such as saving a house deposit – that you want to prioritise?

If you do decide to make a lump sum repayment then aim to do it before June 1 before indexation is applied.

## Build a cash cushion

Make the most of your pay. Keep your expenses low and your savings high. Start by building up an emergency fund so that you don't have to resort to your credit card when your car breaks down or you get a big bill from the dentist. Ideally, aim to have enough money to cover your essential expenses for at least three months but even a few thousand dollars can be a great cash cushion.

## Set your goals

I'm also big on having a vision of what you want to achieve because having something to aim for will give you the motivation to do whatever you need to do to get there. Right now you might just be thinking about repaying debt and building up your cash cushion, but what are your goals for the future?

Do you want to buy a house, go on a three-month European holiday, or plan for a dream wedding? Set short-, medium- and long-term goals and work towards them.

## Start saving

Your goal should be to save as much as you can now. You might be surprised at just how much this can add up to over time, thanks to the magic of compound interest. Say you start putting away just $50 a week when you're 20 and earn an average return of 5%pa. By the time you are 67 you'll have $493,000. Wait 10 years to start saving that money and you'll have about $279,000 – $214,000 less!

I know this can be harder if your friends are big spenders who have a lavish lifestyle and go out five nights a week. I get it – you don't want to miss out. But think of ways you can have a great time without breaking the bank.

Rent an outfit instead of buying a new one each time you have a special night out or borrow from a friend. Take the initiative and make plans that are within your budget rather than letting your friends pick the restaurant.

And if you need some extra cash to help fund a lifestyle you're happy with and still save, then the sharing economy has really made that much easier. Like animals? Sign up to Mad Paws. Spare time? Become an Airtasker. Got a car? Rent out your car using Car Next Door. Better still, if you live in the city, ask yourself if you even need a car! Do your sums and you might be better off using Ubers or a car sharing service rather than owning one.

You could earn even more by combining a few different platforms. Remember, you need to declare the income in your tax return.

## Dial up the risk and invest

Leave your money in a bank account and one thing is for sure: you won't get rich. To avoid your savings going backwards you need to dial up the risk. Over the long term, shares and property are far more effective at creating wealth than cash or fixed interest.

The good news is that through a managed fund or an exchange traded fund (ETF) you can invest indirectly in these asset classes with as little as $500. In a managed fund the manager buys and sells investments regularly in an effort to outperform a specific sharemarket index. An ETF, also known as an index fund, usually buys a portfolio of assets that mimic an index. Look at Chapter 7 ("I'm ready to start investing") for investment options.

# Protect yourself

The most valuable asset you have is your ability to earn an income. If you're 25 and earning $50,000 a year now, you have the potential to earn more than $3.8 million between now and 65, allowing for some pay rises. So while you might not need life insurance if you don't have kids, you really should think about income protection. This pays up to 75% of your income if you're unable to work due to sickness or disability. Premiums are tax deductible.

Another question you might ask yourself is, "Should I get private health insurance?" If you earn over $90,000 or you're 30, it pays to have, at the very least, basic hospital cover. Not only will you save on tax (the Medicare levy surcharge) but you'll end up saving on premiums (lifetime health cover loading). If you don't take out hospital cover before July 1 after your 31st birthday, a 2% loading on your premium will apply each year for every year you don't have private hospital cover.

For example, if you take out cover when you are 40, you may pay 20% more than someone who first took out hospital cover at 30. The maximum loading is 70%. The tax office also charges an extra 1% to 1.5% if you earn $90,000-plus and don't have hospital cover. Why give the tax office this money? Use it to cover yourself.

# Do your future self a favour

Retirement might seem like a long way off but your future self will thank you for the small things you do now.

It's important to understand your rights when it comes to superannuation. If you are employed and aged 18 or over, your employer is required to make regular super contributions on your behalf, currently 10.5% of your salary. This is set to increase to 11% from July 1, 2023.

Most people can choose which super fund their employer's contributions are paid into and your employer will give you the form to enter the details.

Have a say in where your money is invested by choosing a fund option that suits your needs and where you are in life right now, otherwise your employer will choose a MySuper option, which is normally a balanced option.

You may want more in growth assets or you may be more conservative. Some super funds also have member-direct options, which mean you can choose the individual shares to invest in, but this is not for everyone.

# If you only do one thing...

Bank your pay rises.
Each time you get a pay rise,
put the extra money straight
into savings or towards your
investing. You managed without
it before so there's no reason you
need to spend it now!

Your employer's contributions have to be paid into your super account at least quarterly. If you want to check that your employer is making these payments on time, you can generally log into your super account online, or via an app if the fund has one. You may also be able to check by using your myGov account, which will show you how much has been paid into your fund. If you have any doubts, your first port of call should be your employer but, if after talking to them you still have concerns, you can contact the tax office.

Consider making your own contributions as well. Let's say you're 24, earn $70,000 a year and have $25,000 in your super. If you start popping $10 a week into your super, you could enjoy an extra $37,000 by age 67.

And if you're self-employed you don't have to contribute to your super but you might regret not adding to your retirement savings. You can get a tax deduction and pay just 15% on any contributions you make up to the limit.

When you change jobs, your new employer will give you the option to nominate the super fund you want your contributions to be paid into. You can ask them to use your existing fund or you can transfer your super into a new fund. If you don't choose a fund your employer has to pay the super contributions into your existing account – this is referred to as super stapling.

## Big brother is watching

You may not realise that some of the things you do will appear on your credit report. You are entitled to a free copy of your credit report every three months. You can request it from one of the three main credit reporting bodies in Australia: illion, Equifax and Experian. Lenders use the report and your score to assess any applications you make for credit. The information in the report is also used to calculate your credit score.

## Build good habits

Start as you mean to go on. By that I mean learn how to cook so you don't spend all your money on Uber Eats, pack your own lunch to take to work rather than buying it, have the office instant coffee instead of buying a latte each morning. It's much easier to do this from the beginning rather than getting used to your morning chat with the barista or getting hot meals delivered to your door and then having to give them up!

# Checklist

☐ *If you've racked up credit card debt, focus on paying it off fast.*

☐ *Build a cash cushion of at least a few thousand dollars to cover unexpected costs.*

☐ *Set your short-, medium- and long-term financial goals.*

☐ *Start a savings plan to set yourself up for a great financial future.*

☐ *Dial up the risk and invest – it doesn't have to be a huge amount but time is on your side so use that to your advantage and take some chances.*

☐ *Protect yourself by taking out income protection cover.*

☐ *Consider at least basic health insurance if you're over 30 or earn more than $90,000.*

☐ *Take control of your super – know your rights, make sure your employer is paying up, have a say in where your money is invested and make sure you always keep track of fees and performance.*

☐ *Keep an eye on your credit file and credit score.*

☐ *Set good habits that will put you on the path to success.*

## LET'S GET REAL ...

I'll never forget the day my son blew his home deposit savings on an Xbox. He'd been saving for a home for some time but it appears that the pressure of getting together a $180,000 deposit got the better of him. (That was enough for a 20% deposit for a house in Sydney when I first wrote this book in late 2018. As I update it four years later, this has increased to $260,000.)

As he handed over his cash, I reminded him what that money was supposed to be for. He kindly reminded me that he was only 10 and that he had plenty of time to save. Besides, he said, "I'm never going to have enough to buy a home."

I suspect his sentiments are pretty much how most budding first home buyers feel, but you can either sit back and feel defeated or you can face the challenge head on. My first property was bought with the help of my mum and dad (they had the majority of equity but it gave me a foothold on the property ladder). My second property involved selling all my bank shares and my beloved MX5, and then to help fund some major renovations, my partner and I decided to move back into his parents' home. Two blissful years with the in-laws! As they say, no pain, no gain – it got me where I needed to be!

# CHAPTER

# 4

*I'll never own*
*a home*

# Need to know

*Can you believe you might be too old to get a home loan? According to Home Loan Experts, different banks have different policies for borrowers based on age.*

*• 35: Lenders will consider your profession and likely retirement age and they may shorten your loan term.*

*• 45: You may be required to show superannuation statements or demonstrate that you have an exit strategy in place to repay the loan when you retire.*

## MOST AUSSIES ARE OBSESSED WITH OWNING A HOME BECAUSE WE THINK OF IT AS A RITE OF PASSAGE.

In fact, it wasn't too long ago that there was a real expectation that buying a home was something you'd work towards in your 20s or 30s. Not so now, though! Having anything vaguely close to a decent deposit means saving tens of thousands of dollars – that's not easy, especially if you're renting. You may feel as if you'll never be able to own a home but plenty of people beat the challenges, and you can too.

Buying your first home doesn't have to mean living on two-minute noodles and instant coffee for years (although I don't mind instant coffee). The trick is to think outside the square. There's a whole variety of different strategies you can mix and match to get you over the line and into your first home.

## IS HOME OWNERSHIP REALLY FOR YOU?

First up, be sure home ownership is right for you. It's a major commitment – one that could last a lot longer than plenty of marriages.

It's not the end of the world if you choose to rent. Renting can have its advantages. You've got more freedom to move, and if the stove breaks down you just call the property manager to fix it pronto. You don't have to wear the cost and hassle yourself. But, as I write this, we are experiencing a rental crisis with fewer properties available to rent and rental prices skyrocketing, so finding a decent place to rent is not easy.

One of the big pluses of home ownership is that it stacks up financially. It may not feel that way when you're forking out for stamp duty, legal fees and all the other costs that come with buying a home. But over time it puts you in front.

You've probably been told more than once (as if you hadn't already worked it out) that renting is dead money. That's true. But so is paying interest on a home loan. Interest on your home loan makes up a large portion of the payments and that's definitely money heading to the undertaker!

So if you want to come out in front with home ownership, you need to knuckle down and pay off your place as soon as possible. Otherwise, if you run the numbers you may actually find you're better off renting – as long as you're investing, too. And that's the key to it: you must be disciplined enough to keep investing which can be easier said than done when rents are soaring.

Why do I prefer home ownership over renting? It's forced me to save, and the beauty about buying well is that property should grow in value while the balance of your loan is steadily shrinking. Over the past 30 years property prices have more than quadrupled in some locations.

Renting, on the other hand, buys a roof over your head but not much more. As a homeowner, you'll put a fair chunk of cash into the bank's pocket but, ultimately, you will end up with an extremely valuable asset. And that's what makes all the effort of buying a place worthwhile. So let's see how you can do it.

## How much of a deposit do you really need?

You generally need at least a 5% deposit to be able to get a loan but if you borrow more than 80% of the purchase price you may need to pay lenders mortgage insurance (LMI). This protects the lender, not you, if you can't keep up your loan repayments. And the premiums because they can be very high.

As a guide, if you buy a place for $500,000 with a 10% deposit of $50,000, LMI will cost around $8700. With a deposit of just 5%, the premium jumps to about $15,000. You can pay it upfront or add it to your loan, but this means you will pay interest. There are a few ways you may be able to avoid LMI, which I'll look at next.

As well as covering the deposit, you'll also need enough money to cover all the upfront expenses such as stamp duty, legal fees, inspections and bank fees. These can add an extra 5% to 7% to the cost, so it's important to factor these in when setting your savings goal.

## HOW TO AVOID LMI

It is possible get into the market with a smaller deposit and not having to fork out thousands for LMI. Lenders offer special LMI discounts from time to time and may waive LMI for certain professionals such as lawyers, accountants and doctors. It's worth looking out for those. Here are a few more ways to avoid LMI.

## Get family to help with the deposit

Think about asking your mum and dad or other relatives, if they can put some cash towards your deposit to help you hit your 20% goal to avoid LMI. Yes, it means relying on the bank of mum and dad but it happens a lot more than you might realise.

Having a cash gift under your belt might help you avoid LMI but it doesn't get you off the savings hook entirely. Lenders want to know that you have the discipline to handle regular loan repayments, and you'll still be asked for proof of regular savings, usually extending back three to six months.

You may also be asked to provide a letter from your parents stating that the cash they have contributed is a gift and not something they expect to be repaid.

## Use the government's Home Guarantee Scheme

The Home Guarantee Scheme is a government initiative designed to help home buyers purchase a home sooner. It includes the First Home Guarantee, the Regional Home Guarantee and the Family Home Guarantee, all administered by the National Housing Finance and Investment Corporation (NHFIC).

The First Home Guarantee allows eligible first home buyers to buy a home with as little as 5% deposit without paying LMI. The government guarantees up to 15% of the value of the property that you purchase to a participating lender. You will need to meet certain eligibility criteria such as an income test – for singles, your taxable income for the previous income year must not be more than $125,000, or for couples, your combined taxable income for the previous income year must not be more than $200,000. There are also property price caps which vary based on where the property is located. The First Home Guarantee is limited to 35,000 places each financial year.

The Regional Home Guarantee operates in much the same way as the First Home Guarantee but is specifically for first home buyers in regional areas. You can buy a home with as little as 5% deposit and the government will guarantee up to 15%. The same income limits of $125,000 a year for singles and $200,000 for couples apply. The same property price caps in place for the First Home Guarantee also apply here. To qualify, you must have been living in the region for at least 12 months. There are 10,000 spots available each year.

Then there's the Family Home Guarantee which is designed to help eligible single parents with at least one dependent child buy a family home with a deposit as little as 2% and no LMI. The government will guarantee up to 18% of the property's value. To be eligible your taxable income must not have been more than $125,000 for the previous financial year. The property price caps also apply. There are 5000 spots available each financial year.

Visit nhfic.gov.au for more details about eligibility criteria and price caps.

# *Ask your parents to go guarantor*

Your parents may be able to lend a hand in other ways that don't involve dipping into their own pocket. If you don't qualify for any of the government guarantee schemes, and your parents own their home, have a chat with them about acting as a guarantor for your loan. It can be super helpful, especially if you're in a position where you earn enough to pay rent but not enough to save a big deposit as well.

A guarantor puts up the equity in their own home as additional security for your loan. No cash changes hands but this extra layer of security can get you over the line if you have a small deposit.

By taking up the slack from your deposit, your guarantor can also help you avoid LMI. Let's say you have a cash deposit of 5%, and your mum and dad are willing to guarantee 15% of your property's value. The combination of your savings and the backing of your guarantor gives you security equivalent to a 20% deposit. Hey presto, no need for LMI.

Having a guarantor sounds simple enough but there is a serious side to it. If, for whatever reason, you can't keep up your home loan repayments, the lender will turn to your guarantor to pay out the loan. This is why it's important that your guarantor gets legal advice to understand what's involved.

## MAKE A PLAN TO SAVE

So you may only need a 5% deposit to buy a home. At today's prices, even a 5% deposit is a decent bundle of cash, and just skipping a few cappuccinos each week is not going to get you there. It calls for some serious saving power – or a major change in lifestyle.

Look for ways to cut costs or pick up a few side hustles to make extra cash. Check out Chapter 1 ("How can she afford that?") for tips. And if you're renting, moving back home will save you a fortune. If you can channel those savings into your deposit, you'll be well placed to make an offer on a place a lot sooner than you anticipated.

When you have set your target amount, I suggest working backwards to calculate how much you need to save to achieve your goal. Let's say you want to save $50,000 in five years, you'd need to put away $833 a month. This doesn't factor in any earnings but you get the gist.

# If you only do one thing...

Start saving now! $100 per week over 10 years at just 3%pa will see you have $60,555 in your online saver. Double that and you'll have more than enough to put a 20% deposit on a $500,000 home. Where are you going to find $200 a week? Bring your lunch to work and skip dining out on Saturday nights!

# Now where to stash your cash?

The best place to grow your cash depends on the amount you have already saved, how much you can save on a regular basis, the time frame you are looking at and the level of risk you are willing to take.

Many budding home buyers use online savings accounts to stash their cash. The biggest plus of this option is that your money is certainly safe, as the federal government guarantees deposits up to $250,000 in authorised deposit-taking institutions. This is all well and good but it still means that your own regular deposits have to do most of the heavy lifting.

One way to fast-track your deposit is not necessarily to save more but rather to invest it in a way that will see you earn a higher return.

The biggest problem with saving in a cash account is ensuring your deposit keeps up with property price growth.

That's why I like saving using the asset class I want to buy, in this case property. If property prices rise so will your deposit and if they fall so will your deposit. Fractional funds such as the Smart Invest product from fractional home investing platform BrickX are one option, as are property exchange traded funds (ETFs). Just watch for fees.

Or if you want to diversify away from property but still dial up the risk and therefore potential returns, there are ETFs that track, say, the main sharemarket index, the S&P/ASX 200.

There are downsides to this strategy. With ETFs, for example, brokerage fees of around $15-$20 are charged each time you invest in an ETF. Realistically, this means ETFs are only an option if you're okay with just making a few sizeable lump sum trades, perhaps saving in an online account first, then transferring the funds to the ETF when you've got a solid amount.

The other drawback is that if the sharemarket falls the value of your ETF will drop too, taking your deposit with it. Again, that's fine if you've got a long-term time frame for saving for your first home – at least five years.

# First Home Super Scheme

Another way to save for your first home is through the First Home Super Saver (FHSS) scheme. Here's how it works. The FHSS lets first home buyers make voluntary contributions to their super. You can do this via salary sacrifice – that's where part of your pre-tax wage or salary is paid directly to your super instead of you receiving the money as cash in hand – or through after-tax contributions (even if you claim a tax deduction for them).

Under the FHSS you can add up to $15,000 each financial year, or $50,000 in total, to your super to buy your first home. You do have to stick to the standard contribution caps (currently $27,500 per year for concessional contributions).

Then, when you're ready to buy a place, you apply to the tax office for a release of your contributions plus earnings. If you're part of a couple, you can both use the scheme and can pool your savings together. So, together you could potentially release $100,000 (plus earnings).

How does the FHSS help you grow a deposit? The benefit of saving through your super is that your before-tax contributions as well as the investment returns are taxed at only 15%.

Even if you make an after-tax contribution, you can claim a tax deduction to get the benefit too. That's likely to be a lot less than the tax you pay on your wage or salary. So more of your money goes towards growing your deposit instead of paying the tax office. (By the way, contributions withdrawn under the FHSS get a 30% tax offset, so you hold onto the tax savings.)

The catch with the FHSS, though, is that if you change your mind about buying a home, you won't be able to withdraw your contributions to spend on anything else. The money is locked away until you retire.

## Mix and match

There's no single right or wrong strategy when you're saving for a first home. You're free to mix and match. Personally, I like the idea of having some in cash to keep things safe and some in high-growth investments – as long as you have the time and risk appetite.

If you're planning to buy a $600,000 home with a 10% deposit ($60,000), for example, you can choose to save $20,000 in super under the FHSS, $30,000 using an ETF and $10,000 in an online savings account. It's about what works for you.

# Fast fact

A $10,000 *limit on your credit card can reduce the amount you can potentially borrow by* $56,000! *And that's regardless of what you owe. Boost your borrowing power by reducing your limits before you apply for a home loan.*

## MORE OPTIONS TO HELP YOU GET ON THE PROPERTY LADDER

If you are finding it tough to save enough money yourself, don't give up. More solutions are available.

*Rentvesting – get into the market, live where you want*

Maybe you've looked at all the options so far and thought, "Well, yes, but I still can't afford to buy in the area where I want to live." If that sounds like you, you've probably run into the well-meaning types who've explained that their first home wasn't their dream home, and getting into the market is all about compromise.

It's true that a bit of flexibility about where you're prepared to live can go a long way towards getting into the market. But you can only be so flexible with something as important as where you want to live.

There's no doubt that some of the most affordable neighbourhoods are new estates in outer suburbs. They offer good value, with house and land packages that provide a lot of bang for your buck. And that's why they're popular with first home buyers. But they're not for everyone. If you really want to live in an area to be close to friends, family, work or just your favourite cafe, there is a Plan B – rentvesting.

Rentvesting involves buying an investment property that you rent out while you pay rent where you live. It's not a new concept by any means but if you've had your heart set on buying a place to call home, rentvesting can call for a radical change in thinking. It's worth looking into it, though, because it can let you get a toehold in the market while still living in your preferred suburb.

One of the great things about buying as an investor is that you have complete freedom of choice (within the limits of your budget) about where you buy. Your property doesn't need to be close to work or family, so you can consider more affordable suburbs that you maybe wouldn't choose to live in yourself – including interstate or regional locations. Yet these areas can combine affordability, good rent returns and rising property values.

So far, so good. But where will you live? That's where the "rent" part comes into it. Renting is often cheaper than owning in a given suburb, and as a tenant you're free to select the neighbourhood that best meets your preferences.

Do the numbers stack up? As a rentvestor, the rental income you receive helps to cover the costs of owning the place, including loan repayments. Any shortfall between the rent and property-related expenses such as loan interest can normally be claimed on tax. Being able to claim this loss is what "negative gearing" is all about, and it can trim the tax you pay on your regular wage or salary – a saving that can go towards paying rent where you live.

The icing on the cake is that any increase in the value of your investment property can be used to fund a home of your own further down the track. You may not even need to sell the place to benefit from the equity built up in your rental property. In some cases, lenders will accept the equity in your investment property in place of a cash deposit on a home purchase.

As a rentvestor, you won't face maintenance costs on the place you live in – that's the landlord's problem. However, you will be responsible for the upkeep of your own rental property. So be sure your budget can handle ongoing expenses such as insurance, rates and repairs. Plenty of these costs can be claimed on tax but you need the funds to pay for them in the first place.

Something to keep in mind though is that buying as a rentvestor will mean you miss out on the First Home Owner Grant and stamp duty concessions. The two combined can be worth more than $20,000, and that's a decent chunk of money to knock back. But you could find that the tax savings from your rental property far outweigh any first home buyer benefits. And remember, the tax breaks are available year after year, whereas the FHOG is a one-off payment.

One aspect you do need to be aware of is that if you sell a rental place further down the track, any profit on the sale is taxable. Your own home, on the other hand, is tax-free.

Knowing if rentvesting is the right choice for you can come down to crunching the numbers. But it can be a way to enjoy a slice of property market gains while still living in your preferred location.

## Co-buying – combine forces

When you're planning to buy a place on your own, it can feel as if you're being squeezed out of the property market. After all, couples have the natural advantage of having double the purchasing power. But there's nothing to stop you from getting in on the act by pitching in with a co-buyer.

By pooling your resources you may be able to afford a higher-quality property or a better suburb.

If your co-buyer has previously owned a home, you won't be eligible for the First Home Owner Grant yourself. But that may be a minor downside compared with the benefit of a greater combined buying power.

A growing number of lenders recognise that first home buyers often need to buy with a friend or family member, so securing a home loan shouldn't be a problem as long as you both have a good credit record and enough income to meet the repayments.

Nonetheless, I've come across plenty of stories from people who have not enjoyed the co-buying experience. Unfortunately, the more complicated you make your home purchase, the greater the potential for something to go wrong.

And buying a property with someone else is nothing like organising a holiday with your best friend. You'll be sharing a major debt so it pays to be really picky about who you bring into the arrangement. If you have the slightest doubt about a potential candidate's income, their attitude to money and, in particular, the way they handle debt, scratch them from your list.

If you find someone you feel comfortable sharing a home purchase with, the golden rule is to have an agreement – in writing and preferably drafted by a solicitor – that spells out how your set-up will work. It should include how you'll split costs as well as what happens if one person wants out.

A danger with co-buying is that a few years into the arrangement one owner may start to head in a different direction. Even if your written agreement explains the steps to take if your co-buyer wants to bail out of the arrangement, you could still be left high and dry. It could mean you have to put the place on the market at a time when prices are down.

The point is that co-buying is a way of getting into a home of your own if you can't afford to do it solo. Just think it through carefully.

## Take advantage of shared equity schemes

Another way to buy a home if you have a small deposit and still avoid LMI is to use a shared equity scheme. Essentially, these involve getting an equity partner/ investor to chip in some of the purchase price, and in return, they get a stake in the property.

Many state and territory governments are operating these schemes for residents and there are private companies offering shared equity options. And the Albanese government's planned Help to Buy program is expected to cut the cost of buying a home by up to 40%.

With any of these schemes, you will need to contribute some money towards the purchase of the property but in some cases that can be as low as 2%. Not only do these schemes eliminate the need for LMI, they mean you will have a smaller mortgage and therefore lower repayments.

It's important to make sure you look at the fine print to understand the eligibility criteria, the costs involved and what happens when you want to sell.

## Rent to buy

Another option you may consider is a rent-to-buy arrangement. This gives you the option to purchase a property in the future (which can be anywhere from two to seven years) for a price you agree to now. Until then, you have to pay rent for the property but this will generally be higher than market rent and you may have to also pay an ongoing fee.

The advantage of rent-to-buy is that setting the price at the time of purchase provides you with a clear target to work towards. The catch is that if the market falls, you could end up paying more than the place is worth.

However, it can be an extremely risky option. If you can't secure a mortgage when the agreed time is up, for example, you could end up having to walk away and losing any money you have contributed while renting. It's also important to note that with rent-to-buy schemes you don't own the property until it settles.

So this is one option to take extra care with and make sure you know what you're getting yourself into and your rights and responsibilities.

# Checklist

- ☐ *Work out how much you need for a deposit.*

- ☐ *Explore options that may help you buy a home with a smaller deposit without having to pay LMI including asking family for help or government schemes.*

- ☐ *Choose where you'll grow savings. Mix and match between various options.*

- ☐ *Consider rentvesting if you can't afford to buy in the area you want to live in.*

- ☐ *If you can't afford to buy on your own, think about co-buying with a friend or relative or look into shared equity schemes.*

## LET'S GET REAL ...

For a long time, we had it pretty good with interest rates. I mean, back when I was a loans officer for a major bank, interest rates were in the double digits. Yes, property prices have reached nosebleed levels but as far as repayments go, they've been pretty comfortable up until now.

As I write this updated edition, interest rates are rising at their fastest ever pace and the cost of living soared to a 21-year high. Now more than ever Aussies don't want to be living with a mortgage.

Whether rates are high or low, the same money-saving concepts apply – pay more if you can, pay fortnightly instead of monthly and understand that loyalty doesn't pay.

Home loans will always be the bread and butter of banks so competition will be rife, regardless of whether rates are moving up or down. Unfortunately, though, the best deals seem to be reserved for new customers. If you haven't already, pick up the phone and ask your lender what interest rate they are offering to new customers and if you can get that deal. Check out the Bill Buster Action Plan for tips on what to say when you make the call.

# CHAPTER

# 5

*I don't want
to live with
a mortgage!*

# If you only do one thing...

Many Aussies were able to cope when rates started rising because they had built a buffer. Even if the rate on your loan drops, don't reduce your repayments. By continuing to pay the higher repayments you'll not only be repaying your debt faster but you'll build yourself a buffer for when rates inevitably go up again.

## IT'S GREAT TO OWN YOUR OWN HOME – BUT IF YOU TAKE 25 OR 30 YEARS TO PAY IT OFF, THE INTEREST WILL BE A KILLER.

Borrow $500,000 at 4%pa and make no extra repayments and you'll pay a whopping $292,000 in interest over the 25-year loan. If rates were, say, 6% you'd fork out $466,000 in interest. So getting rid of your mortgage quickly is definitely in your best interests.

## HERE ARE MY TOP TIPS FOR GETTING THE MORTGAGE OFF YOUR BACK FASTER

### Know how mortgages work

The important thing to understand about home loans is that interest is calculated on the daily balance and charged to the loan account monthly in arrears. Take advantage of this fact. If you can reduce the daily balance, even by just a few dollars, you will save in the long run on both interest paid and the term of your loan.

In dollar terms: Let's say you have a $500,000 home loan at 6%, where interest is calculated on the daily balance and charged monthly in arrears. Over a 25-year term your repayments would be $3222 a month.

If you make no repayments until the end of January, interest will be calculated each day on a $500,000 balance. Since there are 31 days in January, a total of $2547 in interest would be charged at the end of that month.

Had you made half of your monthly payments on January 15 for example, and the remainder at the end of the month, you would have saved $3.29 in interest at the end of January, which means that an extra $3.29 could have gone towards the principal. The savings may be small but over the long run this will reduce your term and cut a substantial amount off the total interest payable.

### Pay fortnightly

When it comes to slashing your interest bill by a good $86,000 or so (see table on page 66), there is no better strategy (and it's easier too) than paying fortnightly. To get these savings you need to take the minimum monthly repayment, halve it and then pay that amount every two weeks. That's because there are 26 fortnights in a year – the equivalent of 13 monthly repayments rather than 12.

For those borrowers who divide their minimum monthly repayment by four and pay weekly, the savings are slightly higher still on interest but not so much on the term. It's important to note here that some lenders, when calculating fortnightly payments, take the monthly repayments figure, multiply it by 12 and then divide it by 26 to give you a fortnightly amount. While this is correct, it will not reduce your home loan as quickly.

*Example:*

| | MONTHLY | FORTNIGHTLY | FORTNIGHTLY | WEEKLY |
|---|---|---|---|---|
| | | (mth/2) | ([mthx12]/26) | (mth/4) |
| Loan | $500,000 | $500,000 | $500,000 | $500,000 |
| Interest rate | 6% | 6% | 6% | 6% |
| Repayment | $3222pm | $1611pf | $1487pf | $806pw |
| Term | 25 years | 21 years 1 mth | 25 years | 21 years |
| Interest paid | $466,452 | $380,334 | $465,027 | $379,280 |
| Saving | | $86,118 | $1425 | $87,172 |

# Pay extra

The next best thing to fortnightly repayments is making extra repayments. It's the only strategy that can reverse the effects of compound interest in the early years of your loan. There's a simple reason why after the first couple of years you still owe pretty much what you borrowed – only a fraction of your repayments go towards the principal. The rest pay off the interest.

On a $500,000 mortgage at 6% over 25 years your monthly repayments would be $3222 and you'd pay over $466,000 in interest. Round up your repayments to $3300 – so an extra $78 a month – and you'd save nearly $29,000 in interest.

Better still, make fortnightly repayments of $1650 and the savings jump to over $106,000.

# Make one-off contributions

Even if you can't afford to make additional repayments, one-off lump sum deposits such as a tax refund or a small windfall can have a surprising impact.

In dollar terms: A lump sum payment of, say, $1500 in the third year of a $500,000 home loan at 6% could cut your term by two months and save you more than $4000 in interest. Why not deposit your tax refund into your mortgage every year? You'll never miss what you never had.

## Use your savings to reduce interest

Make sure your home loan has redraw or offset. Both reduce the interest you pay but offset is a little more versatile.

An offset is a transaction account that's linked to your home loan. The money you have in this account offsets the amount you owe, and you'll only be charged the interest on the difference. And because no interest is paid to the offset account (as less interest is charged to your loan account), you pay no tax on the savings interest. You can link your offset account to a debit and/or credit card.

You can speed things up by living off your credit card. The idea is that on payday your salary goes into your offset account. You use your credit card for living expenses, taking advantage of the interest-free period. During this time your salary is cutting your home loan interest bill. This strategy only works if you repay your credit card before the interest-free days end.

A redraw facility sits inside your home loan, so it's not a separate account that can be linked to a debt or credit card. Redraw can also have some restrictions: for example, your lender can turn off the facility if your situation changes. Redraw fees and a maximum and minimum for redraws can also apply.

In dollar terms: $5000 sitting in either a redraw or offset account would save you over $17,000 in interest on a $500,000 loan at 6% over 25 years.

## Get the best deal

Even though the cash rate has been increasing, it may still be possible to get a better deal. Comparison sites such as Canstar (of which I am Editor-at-Large) can help you get an idea of what's on offer. You could also use a mortgage broker.

If you do find a better deal, though, don't rush to switch. Ask your current lender if they can beat or match that rate and you can save yourself the hassle (and potential cost) of switching.

If your lender won't come to the party with a cheaper rate, make sure you do a break-even analysis before refinancing. Add up all the costs of moving and divide this by your monthly savings. If, for example, it costs you $1000 to move but you would save $50 a month in repayments, your break-even cost is 20 months, meaning it will take you just under two years to recoup the cost of moving. You also need to ask yourself whether you can be certain that your new lender will be just as competitive then as it is today.

Even if you do refinance to a loan with a lower rate you should try to keep your repayments at the level you were paying for the more expensive loan and you'll save even more.

So let's say you had a $500,000 home loan at 6%pa. Your repayments would be $3222 a month and you'd pay $466,452 in interest. You refinance to a loan at 5.5% and your repayments would be $3070 a month, with $421,131 in interest – a saving of more than $45,000. Stick to paying the $3222 a month you were paying on the 6% loan and you'd save a further $45,877.

## Should you lock in?

It's a question I get a lot: "Should I fix my home loan?" There is no right or wrong answer. If things are already tight and you're worried about how you'd cope if rates increased further, then it can be tempting.

It's important to realise that, typically, you will be paying a premium to lock in. The question to ask yourself is if you're happy to pay that little bit extra for certainty. If the answer is yes and you opt for a fixed loan just make sure it's flexible. The good news is more and more are these days. Some of the key questions to ask are:

• Can you make additional repayments during the fixed term and if so what is the maximum?

• Can you offset the fixed interest charged against savings?

• Can you lock in the advertised fixed rate when you first apply for your loan?

• What is the break cost if you want to pay out the loan early?

If being able to make extra repayments is important to you, you can maximise the extra repayments you can make without being penalised, by splitting your fixed loan into two or even three accounts. This way you double or triple the amount of your penalty-free allowance.

If you're uncertain about locking in you may want to hedge your bets by fixing only part of the loan and leaving the rest variable. But if you are thinking about selling your home any time soon, fixing may not be the best idea as you will have to pay if you break your contract.

# Checklist

☐ *Know how mortgages work and use this to your advantage.*

☐ *Pay your loan off fortnightly instead of monthly.*

☐ *Make extra repayments on your mortgage – either one-off or regularly.*

☐ *Make the most of redraw or offset to reduce interest paid on your loan.*

☐ *Look for the best possible deal but don't switch until you've done a break-even calculation.*

## LET'S GET REAL ...

When you're in love you can make some really dumb money decisions. I blame all the adrenaline, dopamine and serotonin that flood my loved-up brain for all the mistakes I made. All it took was for my partner to say "pretty please" and I said "yes" to him being an additional cardholder on my credit card. At the time it made complete sense. He's a small business owner, so why put him through the painful process of applying for a card when it was easier to just add him to mine – plus I'd get all of his rewards points! Of course, I should have known better. As the primary cardholder, my financial reputation was on the line, not his. I like to pay my bills on time every time; he, on the other hand, is a little more relaxed, and with a variable income likes to set his own pace.

Introducing this card into our marriage was the worst money decision I made. We fought constantly over this card so we closed it. We agreed that for the sake of our financial love life it was best if we kept our personal expenses separate. To this day we pretty much keep our finances separate but our goals united.

# CHAPTER

# 6

*I'm so in love!*

# If you only do one thing...

Say "no" to signing any document that doesn't give you a financial benefit. The only cure for a sexually transmitted debt is to stick your heels in. By all means help your loved one but don't carry all the risk with no reward.

## FINANCIAL STRESS IS ONE OF THE TOP CAUSES OF BREAK-UPS, ACCORDING TO RELATIONSHIPS AUSTRALIA, AND WHILE BILLS, BUDGETS AND DEBT ARE HARDLY THE STUFF OF ROMANCE, COUPLES WHO TALK MONEY HAVE A BETTER SEX LIFE.

Okay, this may not be entirely true. In fact, I couldn't find any research to support it, but I did find that having these tough talks with your partner is the key to a healthier financial relationship.

So how do you start these awkward conversations? If it's a new relationship, going in lightly may be more effective. For example, ask: "What would you do if you won $1 million?" Their answer should give you some insight into what they value and whether they're a spender or a saver. Going straight in with "Do you have a spending problem?" may not work out too well on your first date.

Before you jump into any money talks, it's a good idea to make sure you are both in the right frame of mind. Setting up fiscal date nights can help to break the ice. Bring a bottle of wine, sparkling mineral water or whatever it takes for you two to get into a money mood. While you should never be short on money topics, here are five themed fiscal date nights to get you started.

### 1. CONFESSION NIGHT

Don't panic! I'm not talking about confessing to how many sexual partners you've had but rather letting your loved one in on how much debt you're lugging around.

If a person brings a ridiculous amount of debt into the relationship, who's responsible for it? What would you consider ridiculous? How did this debt come about? The answers to these questions will reveal a lot about your partner. A student debt, for example, is understandable. A debt from an overseas holiday, maybe. A gambling debt? Cause for concern.

The more open you are with how the debt came about, the easier it will be for you two to work through it.

Write down a list of what you owe and the interest you're paying. Put the good debts to one side, then focus on how you intend to pay off the bad ones.

If you can't agree on who pays what, then it may be worth seeking additional help from an adviser or money counsellor. Red flags should pop up if your partner is cagey on the details.

Even good debt like a mortgage needs to be discussed. You don't want to be supporting them at your expense as you build your assets as a couple.

## 2. APPLE PIE NIGHT

Apple pie night is all about how you two lovebirds intend to manage your expenses. How do you share the apple pie? If you intend on sharing a bank account, what's the objective? A joint account can make joint payments such as mortgage, rent and other bills easier to manage. What if one of you earns more than the other? Do you work on a percentage of your salary to put towards your bills? A good compromise can be a joint account for bills and/or investments, and separate accounts for personal savings.

There is no one size fits all when it comes to how you manage your money but it is important to have the conversation. Here are four ways you could handle your cash as a couple.

### What's mine is mine

You keep your earnings separate, as you do with your bank accounts. You may decide on a joint bank account for bills or you may decide to pay the bills directly from your own accounts. You work out what your joint expenses are and decide on how you split the bills – either 50/50 or if your salaries differ you can agree on a percentage of your income. You communicate regularly and support common financial goals. You're mindful that just because you have separate bank accounts you don't spend at the expense of your joint commitments.

### What's mine is yours and yours is mine

You're happy to share everything in a joint account. It works for you because you're able to keep an eye on everything (including your individual purchases). You both have similar spending habits but to avoid any argument you put rules around how much each of you can withdraw before having to consult one another.

Your legal affairs can also be easier with a joint bank account. If one spouse dies, the other will be able to access the funds in a joint account without having to go through the legal system. On the downside, if the relationship ends there's nothing stopping your partner from clearing the account and doing a runner.

# Your shout but it's no favour

One of you is the homemaker or earns considerably less than the other. The main income earner pays this partner an allowance that's transferred to their own account. The value of the allowance depends on what you both agree this money is to be used for. If it's for bills and groceries, then it would be considerably more than if it were just for personal expenses. The allowance is never seen as a favour. You have a joint account for bills which both partners can access.

# I'll take care of that, you take care of this

Perfect for blended families or couples who may have commitments outside their current relationship, such as student debts or another child. Each partner picks a bill or expense that they are responsible for. It doesn't necessarily need to be the same amount. Couples need to agree on how this may affect their ability to reach joint financial goals so as to avoid any arguments down the track.

## 3. ROLE PLAY NIGHT

Not what you're thinking but it can be just as much fun. The idea here is a little like truth or dare. Truth: "If you won $1 million what would you do with it?" If they answer "First-class tickets to Las Vegas, Mercedes-Benz convertible, Ducati and pool for the kids," then you're dealing with a spender. But what if they answered: "I'd give most of it to my mum and dad – after all they raised me!" Will that cause a problem? You'll be surprised at what comes out of role play nights.

*Here are some other questions you can ask:*

• If you had to rate yourself on a scale from 1 to 1000 – 1000 meaning you're great at handling money – what would your score be? Believe it or not, somebody is rating you and if you're about to join your finances together it may be worth knowing what score your partner has. Here are a number of websites that give you access to your credit score free of charge: creditsavvy. com.au, creditsimple.com.au, getcreditscore.com.au, wisrcredit.com.au and clearscore.com.au. As the sites use different data, it can be worth getting your score from both. And you don't have to worry – using these services will not affect your credit file. Your credit score should also go hand in hand with your credit report, also available for free from three main sources. You're entitled to one free credit report from each provider every three months or if an application for credit was declined in the past 90 days. The three main agencies are illion (checkyourcredit.com.au or 1300 734 806), Experian (experian.com.au or 1300 783 684) and Equifax (mycreditfile.com.au or 138 332)

• If your mate Robert asked you for $5000, would you give it to him? Again, the answer to this question will give you an insight into how your partner manages their money. There's nothing wrong with your partner helping out a friend but will they do it properly – because a bad debt will come back to haunt you? I learnt this the hard way. Don't get me wrong: I'm still happy to help out but now I either just gift the money – far easier and I can never be disappointed (it's also good karma) – or if it's a big request I set up a formal arrangement.

## 4. GOAL NIGHT

Does your partner need help putting a plan in place to pay off their credit card? Do you need a little motivation to stop spending? Whatever your money secret, don't be afraid to share it with your partner. Identify what's important to you and what's important to both of you, then put some plans in place to reach your goals. Group them into immediate (under one year), short term (one to three years), medium term (three to five years) and long term (five years or more). If this is overwhelming and it stops you from acting on anything, don't overthink it. Keep it simple, such as saving three months' rent "just in case".

If you're not too sure where to start, then take my Money Makeover challenge (see page 213). Pick any challenge – the easiest one if that gets you started – and together you two can tick off one at a time. I'd be very surprised if you weren't financially better off at the end of it.

## 5. "WHAT IF?" NIGHT

"For richer, for poorer." Sounds reasonable at the time but when the going gets tough many couples choose to go their separate ways. "What if we break up?" is not a ridiculous question to ask. Anyway, it's only hypothetical. Protecting your interest and your partner's interest is best for all, and one way you can both do this is with a prenup. It's even more important if you're coughing up after a divorce, where you've already been through the ravages of a property settlement and you want to protect assets so that you can pass them on to your children from your previous relationship.

# Fast fact

15% of Australians in a relationship don't know how much money their partner earns, according to a survey by Canstar.

# What is a prenup?

A prenuptial agreement is a binding financial contract that allows people to outline what they own and bring to the relationship. In the event of a split-up, it makes it easier to retain their assets, such as the family home, assets for children from an earlier marriage or a family business. It's far easier and cheaper than having to go to the Family Court.

You don't need to be married to draw up a binding financial agreement. They work well for de factos and same-sex couples, too.

You can draw up a binding agreement outlining the assets you want to retain before, during (mid-nuptial) or after (post-nuptial) the relationship.

Not everyone needs a prenup but if you are keen on having one, introduce the idea when you make the decision that the relationship is for the long term. It can be a sensitive topic but it will allow you to see if your partner is open to the idea. It provides an opportunity to talk about your goals and circumstances, and to gauge your partner's response. It is not a good idea to leave it until the wedding is imminent.

# De facto rights

People who live together and are not married are treated the same way by the Family Court as a married couple would be. To be able to pursue a property settlement they must meet at least one of four criteria:

- They were in a de facto relationship for at least two years.
- There is a child of the de facto relationship.
- The de facto relationship was registered in a state or territory.
- When property and assets are assessed, it is found that one party has made significant contributions, and that if an order is not issued, it would be a serious injustice to that party.

# Checklist

☐ *Set up your fiscal date nights.*

☐ *Be open and honest about how much debt you're bringing to the relationship.*

☐ *Share, divide or separate? Agree on how you plan to set up your accounts.*

☐ *Respect your partner's money personality.*

☐ *Set goals – you can work independently as long as you're working towards the same goals.*

☐ *Protect yourself from the unexpected.*

## LET'S GET REAL ...

I keep things pretty simple and that works out just fine for me. Making money is about buying good-quality assets and holding them for a reasonable amount of time. If you can ride out the bumps then you should end up pretty well. As for where to invest, don't over-complicate things. There really are only a handful of options you can invest in – yourself, cash, fixed income, shares and property. There's nothing mysterious about these asset classes. The worst thing you can do is catch investor paralysis. If you think FOMO (fear of missing out) is bad, jumping into an investment because you feel you have to – FOI (fear of inaction) – can be just as bad.

My first real investment was buying as many bank shares as I could afford. That was back in the mid-1990s when I was still wet behind the ears. Was I confident in investing in shares? No. But I did know that it was better to own the bank than have money in it. This paid off well because I later used that investment to help buy my second property.

# CHAPTER

# 7

## I'm ready to start investing

# Need to know

*Fees matter. If you paid 3% in ongoing fees, 59% of your investment would be lost to fees over 30 years, according to research by InvestSMART.*

## YOU MAY BE A BRILLIANT MONEY MANAGER WITH HEALTHY SPENDING HABITS, A REALISTIC BUDGET AND NOT MUCH DEBT, BUT IF YOU'RE NOT INVESTING YOU'RE NEVER GOING TO REALLY MOVE AHEAD FINANCIALLY.

Sounds harsh but investing puts your money to work so you need to do less of the heavy lifting. The good news is that investing is easy.

The crazy part is that investing isn't something women talk about much. But we should because it turns out we're naturally good at it. There's no shortage of research showing women tend to be better at researching different investments than men. We're more likely to be sceptical about sales spins promising a quick buck, and we have a habit of committing to an investment for the long term whereas men will chop and change, chasing high returns.

One piece of research I came across even showed women who invest generally earn higher returns than men. Girl power at its best!

What holds a lot of women back is not knowing where to invest and how to go about it. So let's fix that, so you can get started as an investor.

## Where to invest

Forget everything you've picked up about investing from *The Wolf of Wall Street*. Real-life investing isn't about stock fraud, money laundering or getting wasted on trips to Switzerland. Maybe if it was a whole lot more people would rush out to invest. But that's not the case.

Investing is about setting some goals and choosing the investments that let you achieve them. It also involves knowing how you feel about risk because while we all want to earn juicy returns different types of investments are riskier than others. The higher the potential returns, the greater the risk that you could lose money. It's one of the basic rules of investing. So if you come across anything promising high returns for little or no risk, it's a fair bet you're looking at a scam. Give it a miss.

There's a huge selection of investments to choose from but most fall into one of four main types: cash (which I looked at in Chapter 2 "How much should I be saving?"), fixed interest, shares and property. Of course, there are plenty of other options. Some are more complex than others and that can make it hard to understand how you'll make money, let alone the risks involved. So stick with the basics.

# FIXED-INTEREST INVESTMENTS

As the name says, fixed-interest investments let you earn a set return for a given period. That's quite different from a savings account, where the rate your money returns will fluctuate in line with market rates. And because you're committing to locking your money away, fixed-interest investments usually pay a higher return than savings accounts. The downside is that if rates rise, the return on your fixed-interest investment won't change, leaving you stuck with a lower return.

Fixed-interest investments cover a wide variety of options, including government bonds, which you can invest in through the Australian Securities Exchange (ASX). When you invest in a bond, you are essentially lending money to the issuer of the bond. So, if you buy a government bond you are lending money to the government. You'll receive interest payments (also known as coupon payments) at regular intervals. You'll then get your principal back on the "maturity" date. (You would have been told this date when you made the investment.) You can sell your investment before the maturity date but you may not get the full amount you paid. It depends on what the market value is when you want to sell.

For most people, though, a term deposit held with a bank or credit union is the easiest fixed-interest option. As with a savings account, term deposits are very secure but the value of your money won't grow over time and the returns are low. They can be a great idea if you don't trust yourself not to raid a regular savings account, and if you need cash urgently some banks will let you break into a term deposit early. It will mean being penalised on interest earnings so it's a good idea to only lock away money you don't expect to need during the fixed term.

# SHARES

It'd be easy to assume that residential property is the nation's favourite investment. But that's not the case. According to the ASX Australian Investor Study 2020, Australian direct shares are by far the most widely held asset class, owned by 58% of investors. That compares to just 38% of investors who hold residential investment properties

You don't have to be a stockmarket guru to be a successful investor. The whole idea behind shares is very simple. When you buy a share you're buying a small slice in a business – be it Woolworths, Qantas, one of the banks or a mining company.

As a shareholder, you have the potential to earn two types of income – dividends and capital gains. Dividends are basically your share of the profits and are usually paid once or twice a year. How much you'll receive will depend on how many shares you own. So let's say you own 1000 shares in a company that is paying a dividend of 10 cents per share. This means you'll be paid $100.

Then there are capital gains. If the business does well, it will grow over time, and this will see the value of its shares grow too.

The downside is that shares can rise and fall in value, sometimes dramatically over short periods. That's great when the market is heading upwards but not so much fun when it tanks. That's when a lot of investors become spooked and sell for a loss but sometimes holding on to your investment and riding things out can be a better strategy.

In the past, after a market downswing, shares in decent companies have recovered their value over time and gone on to greater heights. The general trend over time is for values to head upwards. That's why it's important to take a long-term view (at least five years). This way you allow time for your investment to recover from any possible downswings.

Despite the volatility, shares have a lot going for them. They're very low maintenance (no Sunday morning phone calls from a tenant complaining that the hot water heater has exploded) and you don't need much cash to get started.

The ASX recommends starting with around $2000. That way the cost of brokerage, which applies when you buy or sell, is a small proportion of the value of your trade.

Coincidentally, brokerage is super cheap – and could be less than $10 for a $10,000 trade. And getting started with a broker is even easier – just choose one, set up a linked account and you're pretty much ready to go.

Then pick up a few more shares each month, quarter or whenever you have the money. If you trade more frequently or in small amounts, the cost of brokerage will add up but it doesn't hold a candle to the cost of buying or selling a rental property.

If you need cash in a hurry, you can sell all or part of your shareholding and have the cash in your bank account in 24 hours.

The big dilemma with shares is that there are over 2000 companies listed on the ASX. How do you know which ones are decent? It's a question that stumps plenty of people, and that's where exchange traded funds offer a simple and cheap solution.

## EXCHANGE TRADED FUNDS – *instant diversification*

Let me start by saying that diversification is another one of the golden rules of investing. It means spreading your money around so that a handful of duds don't drag down your other investments.

The problem for individual investors is that even if you like the idea of investing directly in shares or property, it's hard to achieve diversification without bucketloads of cash. The solution can be exchange traded funds (ETFs). Think of them as a way to invest in dozens, if not hundreds, of different shares, all for a single upfront price.

When you invest in an ETF, you don't own the shares yourself – you are a unitholder. You are still entitled to a share of the profits through distributions, which are essentially the ETF version of dividends. The other way you can make money on ETFs is through an increase in the value of your units. Let's say you bought 100 units in an ETF for $15 per unit, therefore spending $1500. If 12 months later those units are worth $20, you could sell your investment for $2000, making a capital gain of $500 (excluding brokerage).

Most ETFs follow a 'passive' approach to investing also known as 'index' investing. Essentially, ETFs aim to mirror the returns of a given market index. So, if an index rises 5% in a year, you'd expect the units in an ETF to climb in value by around 5%. The reverse also applies. If the index drops 5%, the ETF's units are likely to experience a similar decline in value.

You may be wondering why just match market returns? Why not aim to do better? Well, for one outperforming investment markets isn't easy. Also, this approach means there's no second-guessing the market, no heavy-duty research and a lot less trading of investments by the fund. Because of all this, ETFs can afford to charge super low fees.

# If you only do one thing…

See a financial adviser
at least once in your life.
Just be sure that they have no
ownership links or affiliations
with product manufacturers
and that they don't receive
commissions or incentive
payments from the products
they refer you to.

There are plenty of ETFs to pick from, and because they're ASX listed you can buy them in much the same way as shares through an online broker. Some focus on the biggest companies on the ASX, others invest in tech companies or overseas companies. There are even ETFs that cover commodities, fixed interest and gold.

With a smorgasbord of ETFs to pick from, you can mix and match to build your own buffet – maybe an ETF with international shares for entree, another with Aussie shares for mains and perhaps a fixed-interest ETF for dessert. That's portfolio diversity sorted.

## ROBO ADVICE – *another way to invest*

If you want some extra help choosing a portfolio of ETFs, one option is online advice or robo advice.

It can all sound a bit Terminator but robo advice is really just automated advice delivered by a computer program. To get started, you provide a few details about your investment goals, how long you plan to invest for and how you feel about risk and, hey, presto, the robo advice service comes up with your ideal portfolio – often based on managed funds and ETFs. From here the computer finetunes your portfolio over time, buying or selling so that your portfolio stays on track to achieve your goals.

Naturally, you can expect to pay for robo advice. However, it can be surprisingly cheap.

If automated investing sounds right for you, take a look at some of the big names in robo advice including InvestSMART (I sit on the board as an independent director), Six Park, StockSpot and QuietGrowth.

## *Getting started in the sharemarket with less*

Even if you don't have a few thousand upfront, it is possible to start investing using smaller amounts thanks to micro-investing platforms such as Raiz, CommSec Pocket, Spaceship Voyager, Pearler and Sharesies. They all operate differently and the minimum investment amounts vary. Let's take a look at a couple in greater detail.

Raiz lets you invest with just $5. It is probably best known for its round-up feature. This basically rounds up your transactions to the nearest dollar and invests the spare change into your Raiz account. You can also make regular deposits. There are seven readymade portfolios to choose from which are made up of varying blends of ETFs. One even gives you exposure to Bitcoin. Raiz also offers an option that lets you build your own custom portfolio. Most Raiz portfolios charge a flat fee of $3.50 per month. Once your investment grows to $15,000, you'll pay fees of 0.275% annually. Bear in mind, the underlying ETFs charge their own management fees which you'll have to pay.

You'll need at least $50 to get started with CommSec Pocket but can build that up over time with regular investments. You can choose from seven ETFs, each with its own theme. Examples include Aussie Top 200, Global 100 and Tech Savvy. You'll have to pay a brokerage fee of $2 each time you invest or sell up to $1000. Trades over $1000 are charged at 0.20% of the trade value. You'll also be charged a management fee by the ETF provider. This will be deducted from the ETF's unit price – it's not an out-of-pocket fee.

It's important to pay attention to the fees as they can easily eat into your investments.

## Property – ARE YOU REALLY READY FOR THE COMMITMENT?

Let's face it, Australia is a nation of real estate junkies. There are whole websites, books, magazines and even apps devoted to investing in real estate. Property values are constantly reported in the media, and it's always a hot topic around office water coolers and backyard barbies. But that doesn't mean everyone is in on the landlord gig.

An investment property will let you earn rent, and over time the value of the place should grow to give you a capital gain.

Buying a rental place is a solid financial commitment. You're going to need to take on a major loan to buy the property, and that's something not everyone is comfortable with – or qualifies for.

# Fast fact

*For the price of one mani and pedi you could have $10,000 invested and managed through a robo adviser for one whole year.*

And don't expect to only have to save a deposit. A huge chunk of your purchase budget will be gobbled up by buying costs such as stamp duty, legal fees, loan application fees and pre-purchase building inspections. These can amount to tens of thousands of dollars, and none of it adds a cent to your property's value. It's literally money to line someone else's pockets. The cash outflow doesn't end there. As a landlord, you'll be expected to maintain the place, and you can expect to wave goodbye to a steady stream of dollar bills that go towards paying:

- *Council rates*
- *Land tax (which doesn't apply to your own home)*
- *Insurance*
- *Maintenance and repair bills*
- *Renovations and improvements*
- *Property management fees, unless you manage the place yourself*

All this adds up. Then when you go to sell your investment property you can expect to pay more legal fees, plus the selling agent's commission along with their marketing bill.

By now you're either pouring yourself a very stiff drink or tearing up the "Homes for sale" section of your local newspaper. Or both. The point is, property is not a bad investment. But it certainly isn't cheap or hassle-free. Why, then, do we get so fired up about the idea of owning a rental place? Easy. Property is something we all know and understand. We can see it and touch it, and even if the market tanks, the building is still standing, still worth something, and still able to be rented by tenants.

There's another reason property is so appealing as an investment: it offers tax savings. And who doesn't love to trim their tax bill?

*Here's how it works.*

If the annual costs of owning your rental property outweigh the rent you earn, you'll make a loss. This loss can be claimed on tax. That's the basis of negative gearing, and it means that owning a rental place can let you cut the tax paid on your regular wage or salary. Or think of it this way: negative gearing means the government (and your tenant) help to pay for your investment. Very few other investments offer this advantage.

Let's ignore the tax perks for a minute, though, to help you decide if a rental property is right for you. Sure, making a loss on your rental property each year can mean tax savings. But a loss is still a loss, and no one gets rich by making losses year after year.

Not only do you need to be able to pay for all the expenses on your investment property, you also need to be sure that the capital growth on the place makes up for these yearly losses. And that's why it's so important to choose the type of property and the suburb you invest in with care.

Buy with your head, not your heart, and look for an area with real growth potential. Look for a growing population, lots of renovation action, plenty of local employment opportunities and decent transport links. Of course, these are exactly the areas everyone else wants to buy in so you may not grab a bargain. But that's not a bad thing. Buying a cheapie because your budget is super tight could mean being lumbered with a property that attracts problem tenants in a go-nowhere neighbourhood.

Before you get all starry-eyed about the thought of owning a rental property, do the sums. Work out if you can really afford to own a place, even when it's vacant for a long period, or if the tenant wrecks the joint, or you lose your regular job, or if interest rates rise.

## What about a fraction of a property?

Maybe you can't afford a whole property but you can pick up a stake in a place (for a fraction of the cost) with "fractional investment" options.

The idea is that an investment property is divided into different slices or units. You can own one or 100 of these slices depending on your budget, and the ongoing costs of each property are paid for out of the rental returns from tenants. You can usually sell your share in the place at any time.

It's a way into the market and if it appeals to you, take a look at fractional investing platforms such as BrickX and DomaCom. Be sure to factor in fees as the smaller your balance the bigger the impact.

# *What about a* FINANCIAL ADVISER?

By this stage, you have a better idea of the main types of investment options and how to get started. Investing is not hard or complicated – and remember, women have a natural knack for it, so don't be afraid to put yours to work.

If you're still not sure, one option is to speak with a financial adviser. But tread carefully. Recommendations and qualifications are your starting points.

Tailored financial advice doesn't come cheap. So even if you find a decent adviser you're comfortable with, be prepared to shell out for advice on steps you could just as easily take yourself – like setting some personal goals and building a portfolio of investments to match. And, frankly, if you just want to kick-start an investment portfolio, you can do the whole thing without outside help.

Sure, if you've just inherited a multimillion-dollar fortune then some professional advice can be a good thing. Or if you're facing some major – and potentially complex – milestones such as retirement, expert advice can be helpful as long as you can wear the cost.

If you are keen on speaking with a financial adviser, consider looking for one who is a member of the Profession of Independent Financial Advisers (PIFA) or the Financial Planning Association of Australia. Both sites have a tool that can help you find members in your area.

# WHEN SHOULD YOU START INVESTING? *Now!*

I'm not worried about what you invest in (unless it's a very suspect offer that's come through an out-of-the-blue email). What I am concerned about is that you keep putting off getting started.

It's not hard! And you know what? After that first trade of shares or units in an ETF you'll realise just how easy it is. Nothing breeds success like success – so go ahead, work out what your goals are, where you want to invest and start spreading your money across a whole range of different opportunities. I can't guarantee you'll always pick a winner. That's investing. But if you choose your investments with care, over time your wins will far outweigh your gains, and your money will be humming along doing plenty of the hard yards on your behalf.

# Checklist

☐ *Set some goals to work towards –
a holiday, a first home, your kids' education
or retirement.*

☐ *Work out the investments that match your
goals – use savings accounts for short-term
goals only.*

☐ *Educate yourself about how different
options work.*

☐ *Spread your money across a variety of
investments. That way any duds won't
ruin all your good work.*

☐ *Be prepared to ride out the storms.
Investment markets don't always
head upwards.*

☐ *Consider getting help – it could be from a
financial adviser or from a robo adviser.*

## LET'S GET REAL ...

Twenty or so years may have passed but I haven't forgotten the decision I made when I was a wet-behind-the-ears graduate trainee for one of the major banks. My first day involved a financial planner discussing the merits of popping extra cash into super. I would have been about 21. Who cares about super when you're that young? I certainly didn't, but my good mate Darren did. He was quite happy to put away $50 each pay. When I think about it now, it really wasn't that much of a sacrifice – a cup of coffee a day. Unfortunately, I lost contact with Darren when I moved from the Gold Coast to Sydney but to this day I wonder how his super is doing compared with mine. Of course, I am salary sacrificing now. As a 50-plus-year-old woman in her peak earning years, I'd be mad not to be taking advantage of the tax perks that come with super.

CHAPTER

Who's got spare cash
to contribute to super?

# If you only do one thing...

If you're salary sacrificing, be sure to crunch your numbers each time the Super Guarantee rate increases. You may need to reduce the amount you are salary sacrificing. As your boss will be adding more to your fund you don't want to risk going over the concessional contributions cap.

## THERE ARE PROBABLY A MILLION PRESSING MONEY ISSUES YOU HAVE TO DEAL WITH RIGHT NOW AND SUPER MIGHT BE LAST ON YOUR LIST. BUT TRUST ME ... YOU REALLY NEED TO MOVE IT CLOSER TO THE TOP.

There's no denying that there is a real gender gap when it comes to super. Even though the gap has slowly been reducing, the statistics are grim. Women retire on average with around 23% less super than men, according to ASFA.

There are a number of reasons for the shortfall. Women earn 14% less than men, they take career breaks to have children, and they work part time to accommodate family commitments. Until recently some women with part-time or casual jobs missed out on super guarantee contributions altogether because there was a $450 monthly minimum threshold for payments. This was scrapped as of July 1, 2022. It also doesn't help that, according to the Workplace Gender Equality Agency (WGEA), higher-paid management opportunities were almost exclusively (90%) for full-time workers while at no age were more than 50% of women working full-time.

Research conducted by Rest, one of Australia's biggest super funds, in 2018 found that taking career breaks costs women almost $160,000 in retirement savings compared with those who took none. Rest also predicts that women who have taken a career break will retire with an average super balance that is $283,000 less than that of their male counterparts.

Has this moved super up on your priority list? If not, how about this? Love it or loathe it, super is (for most of us) one of the most tax-effective wealth-creation strategies for the future. Let me explain why: on a 39% marginal tax rate (including 2% Medicare) you'd pay $390 tax on $1000. However, if you salary sacrifice the $1000 into super, you'd pay just $150 because contributions are taxed at 15%. Why give the tax office an extra $240 when you can "pay yourself forward" by putting it into your super fund?

And if you still need more convincing, maybe this will do the trick. What if I told you there are ways you can boost your super without paying a cent? It might be hard to believe but it is possible. Here's what you need to do.

# Know where your super is

Hands up if you have had more than one job or have moved house and forgotten to tell your super fund! There's a chance you might be one of the millions of Aussies with a lost super account. The tax office is holding billions of dollars' worth of lost super. Finding out if some of that money might be yours is fairly simple. You'll need a myGov account that is linked to the tax office. You can click on the ATO section and go to the "super" tab. There you will see details of all your super accounts, including any you have forgotten about. Visit ato.gov.au/superonline for tips or you can always contact your super fund for help.

# Consolidate your super funds — maybe

Keeping your super in one place can be a good idea because it will mean you're only paying one set of fees, and it reduces paperwork. I say "maybe" because sometimes it's worth having multiple funds if there are distinct benefits, such as cheap life insurance. Or if you have a defined benefit, you should definitely hang onto that. Get an expert to check this for you.

If you are juggling a few super funds, then be aware that you're paying multiple fees, which can erode your hard-earned savings. Fees can eat away at your money, and if you've got one or more inactive accounts, you're missing out on a valuable contribution to your retirement. Super funds with balances of less than $6000 will have administration and investment fees capped at 3% a year, but they still add up.

# Give your fund a health check

At least once a year – when you get your statement, for example – review your fund and make sure it is still the right option for you. How has it performed? Make sure you focus on longer-term returns over at least five years. When looking at performance figures it's important to use the same start and finish dates for each fund. Even one month can make a difference, depending on how markets have performed. Also make sure you're comparing the same type of investment option – don't compare a growth option with one that invests in international shares, for example.

# Check what fees you're paying

As part of your fund's health check, look at the fees you're paying. The main ones are the investment management fee and the administration fee. The management fee is usually a percentage of your balance and varies for different investment options. Then there's the administration fee, which is typically an annual flat "member fee" plus a percentage of your balance. Other costs include entry fees, extra contribution fees, investment strategy switching fees and insurance premiums.

All funds charge fees but some are higher than others, and you might be surprised what effect those fees will have on your balance.

As a guide you shouldn't be paying any more than about 1% on a balanced fund but consider performance after fees as well, as a fund with higher fees might still have performed consistently better than one with lower fees.

# Consider your asset allocation

One of the biggest mistakes people make is being too conservative. If time is on your side, think about taking on more risk and going for a growth option. This decision will depend on your attitude to risk and the time frame you have in mind for retirement but it's something you need to actively think about – don't just let your money sit in the default option. There may be multisector options such as conservative, balanced, growth and high growth or you may be able to choose a specific asset class such as Australian or international shares. Some funds may also let you choose a "mix" – for example, 50% in balanced and 50% in Australian shares.

# Check what insurance you have

Taking out insurance cover in super – including death, total and permanent disability (TPD) and income – can be attractive because the premiums are paid from your super account so the cost doesn't come from personal cash flow.

Some common mistakes, however, are made when arranging insurance through super. One of these is not considering the effect the premiums will have on the balance at retirement because some of your contributions will go towards paying for the insurance rather than being invested to help your money grow.

While the solution is to try to contribute extra amounts to cover the premiums, you should speak to an expert to ensure that you have the right amount of insurance – not too much and not too little – as your super balance is paying for it. For example, you may need more if you have a family or less if you have no dependants.

It's also worth noting that if you take out income protection through your super fund you won't be able to claim a tax deduction for the premium.

## Make sure your employer is paying up

Your employer is required to pay 10.5% of your salary into your super account at least quarterly. This will increase to 11% from July 1, 2023. But Industry Super Australia estimates that almost 3 million workers were shortchanged their compulsory entitlements, at an average of $1700 each or about $5 billion in total, in 2018-19.

You can wait for your statement but it's probably better to keep an eye on things before that. Most super funds have an app or website you can use to confirm that payments are being made. If you can't see your contributions, have a chat to your employer first. If you're not satisfied with the response, you can lodge an inquiry with the tax office.

## Get your spouse to cough up

The bonus is you might both benefit. If you earn less than $37,000, your spouse can contribute up to $3000 a year into your account and in return they get a tax offset of 18% (or up to $540). They might be eligible for a partial offset if you earn less than $40,000.

Longer term there's super splitting, where your spouse can split up to 85% of their before-tax contributions with you. These can be particularly useful strategies to keep building super if you're on maternity leave.

## Talk to your boss

If you're taking time out of the workforce after having a baby, consider asking your employer if they would still make super guarantee payments while you're on parental leave.

# Need to know

Super is not treated the same
way as the rest of your estate,
so if there is someone in particular
you want your super to go to when
you die make sure you set up
a binding nomination and
update it as needed.

According to WGEA, of the employers offering paid parental leave, 81% pay superannuation for parents while on paid leave: 74% pay superannuation during the employer-funded parental leave, and 7% pay superannuation on both employer-funded and government-funded parental leave as well.

## Check whether your fund offers any parental leave perks

Ask your fund if it offers any perks while you are on parental leave. Some will waive insurance or administration fees or refund member fees, for example.

## Get your super topped up when you shop

Consider linking your super fund to a cashback site such as Super Rewards or Boost your Super. Every time you shop through the site you will get cash rewards paid into your super account. The cashback rewards are usually about 2% to 3% but can sometimes be as high as 10%.

## Making extra contributions

Technically you don't have to put in any extra to build your super but your future self will thank you if you do – and a little can go a long way. Let's say, for example, you're 35, earn $80,000 and have a super balance of $50,000. Make no extra contributions and at retirement you'd have $466,083. Salary sacrifice just $15 a week and you'll enjoy an extra $31,093 when you retire.

There are two types of contributions – concessional and non-concessional. Concessional contributions are pre-tax payments that are taxed at 15% going into the fund. They include your employer's contributions as well as any money you "salary sacrifice", which means you get your employer to put it into your super for you before you pay tax on it. Then there are non-concessional contributions, which are those made with money on which you have already paid tax and are not taxed on the way into the fund.

This is where things get a little confusing. You may be able to make a personal contribution and claim a tax deduction. If you're aged 67 to 74 you will need to meet the work test to be able to make a contribution and claim a deduction. You might think that's a non-concessional contribution because you made it from your take-home pay but claiming the tax deduction changes it to a concessional contribution.

# Fast fact

*Fees can make a big difference to your super balance. Let's say a 25-year-old has an average initial income of $77,948 and there's annual inflation of 2.5% on average and average investment returns of 6.85% a year. Canstar calculations show someone paying fees that are 0.75% of their super balance can end up with $165,423 more at retirement than someone paying 1.5%.*

# Understand the caps

If you top up your super make sure you stick to the contribution limits or the penalties can be pretty hefty – as high as 46.5% on the excess amount!

There are different limits depending on whether it's a concessional or non-concessional contribution. You can make up to $27,500 a year in concessional contributions. This limit includes the compulsory contributions made by your employer, so make sure you take that into account when calculating how much you can salary sacrifice so that you don't go over your cap.

For non-concessional contributions, the maximum is $110,000 a year. If you're under 75 and your super balance is less than $1.48 million you may be able to take advantage of the bring-forward rule which lets you make up to three years' worth of non-concessional contributions ($330,000) in a single year.

# Get a government top-up

If you earn under $42,016 and make an after-tax contribution of $1000 to your super, then the government will give you $500. That's a guaranteed 50% return on your money! In fact, if you earn between $42,016 and $57,016, you will receive part of the $500.

# If you're self-employed

If you have your own business or are self-employed, make sure you don't neglect your super as part of your retirement plan. Put money into your super account regularly, just as you would set aside money to pay for GST. You will be able to claim a tax deduction for any contributions you make.

# Checklist

- [ ] *Track down any super you may have "lost" when you moved house or changed jobs.*

- [ ] *If you have more than one super fund, consider consolidating them to save fees and reduce paperwork.*

- [ ] *Give your fund a health check – how has it performed and what are the fees?*

- [ ] *Ask yourself if your money is invested in the right option for your age and risk profile.*

- [ ] *Take a good look at any insurance you're paying for within the fund and if you really need it.*

- [ ] *Check up on your employer to make sure you're being paid what you're entitled to.*

- [ ] *Get your spouse to top up and they may benefit too.*

- [ ] *Ensure your fund has your tax file number.*

- [ ] *Make extra contributions but don't go over the caps.*

- [ ] *Get the government to top you up too.*

- [ ] *Don't neglect your super if you're self-employed.*

## LET'S GET REAL ...

I have two beautiful children who love each other dearly but I'll never forget the day when the eldest said to the youngest that he was a mistake (harsh, I know). Trouble is at that time she didn't realise that she was in fact the "surprise". My first pregnancy was not planned so undoubtedly it took me by surprise. Was I ready for motherhood? Could we afford a child? We need a bigger home! What about my career? This is what I was thinking when two red lines appeared on my pregnancy stick. If I could go back to my 31-year-old self I would say, "Stay calm – all will work out, so just enjoy this miracle you've been given." My surprise is now my greatest joy. Thank you, Nicky, for coming into my world!

If you've never thought about money before, a surprise pregnancy will certainly shift you into financial gear. It is surprising what you're capable of doing if it's a matter of survival. For me, I stopped the Louboutins, the expensive Saturday night dinners and the visits to Scanlan Theodore. Okay, I've had a few lapses at Scanlan since then but only when I could afford to. I chose to go back to work after three months of maternity leave. This was a personal choice and by no means was it easy. As a working mum you will always question yourself. But know that you are not alone. All mums, regardless of whether they are in paid work or not, do. It's something mums are great at!

# 9

*Help, I'm pregnant!*

# If you only do one thing...

While you are pregnant, practise living on one salary, even if for most of the time you have two. This will get you into the habit of being thrifty and hopefully help to pay even more off your home so you have a large buffer for emergencies.

## HAVING A BABY CAN BE VERY EXCITING BUT IT CAN ALSO BE VERY EXPENSIVE.

That first year can be especially tough, especially with the drop from two incomes to one if one partner takes parental leave. That's why it pays to be financially prepared for the pitter-patter of little feet – it will certainly make things less stressful.

If you find yourself unexpectedly pregnant, try not to stress – you do still have about nine months to get things in order. Unless, of course, you're one of those women I've read about who go to hospital with stomach pains only to be told they're in labour. If that's the case, I'm sorry, I can't be of much help!

## Make a list of expenses

First things first … sit down and think about how much it will cost you.

When women fall pregnant they often worry about the cost of a private obstetrician. That's natural – we all want the best care for our baby. I did use a private obstetrician and paid big bucks for it but a co-worker of mine has four kids and all of them were delivered in the public hospital system. Cost: zero.

The choice between going private or public is a personal one and it's not one I'll get into here. If you are going to opt for a private obstetrician, though, make sure you understand all the costs involved with that and what, if anything, private health insurance may cover. Even if you have private health cover you could end up with unexpected additional costs because of the dreaded "gap".

Having a child involves a lot more than booking an overnight stay in the delivery suite of your local private hospital. The best way to plan for the additional bills that a new family member will bring is to draw up a revised "family" budget. The remarkable thing about children, however, is that they have a habit of changing our lives in ways we never expected – and this will flow through to your post-baby living costs.

Yes, you'll need to budget for the essential hardware – prams, high chairs, cots and car seats – as well as software – nappies, formula (if you're not breastfeeding), more nappies, teething rings, emergency nappies and nappy bags. (Did I mention you'll be spending a lot on nappies?) All these can quickly add up to thousands of dollars.

Of course, there are ways to get ready on the cheap – you don't have to buy the most expensive items in the store. Buy second-hand or borrow from friends who've recently had babies.

Keep an eye out for specials. Register for newsletters from your favourite stores and take the time to flick through the catalogues that land in your letterbox, instead of tossing them straight into the recycling bin.

And don't go crazy on clothes – babies don't have to wear designer threads. Sure, you may want one or two nicer pieces for special occasions, but babies grow so fast and you may be surprised how often you need to change them each day thanks to little vomits and other "explosions", so it's really not worth the money.

There's a great calculator at babycenter.com/babycostcalculator that can help you estimate the costs in the first year.

You should also think about whether you need to make any other changes ahead of bub's arrival. For example, do you need to get a bigger car or renovate or move to a bigger home?

The good news is that many of your old costs will change – if not disappear altogether. All-night dinner parties, spur-of-the-moment getaways, ridiculously expensive but absolutely essential high heels – they're all likely to become distant memories for a while. Maybe only for five to 10 years ... and you won't need to spend a fortune on fine arts because your home will be decorated with your child's priceless stick drawings ("Are Mummy's legs really that stumpy, darling? Oh, I see, it's Daddy ...").

## What money will be coming in?

So you have worked out what it will cost you – the next step is to think about what money you'll have coming in. This may help work out how long you can comfortably afford to take off work.

First, find out what you're entitled to, if anything, from your employer. Many larger organisations offer paid parental leave while smaller employers may not have a paid option. How much leave and pay entitlement you get from your employer comes down to your job contract. Most employees in Australia are eligible for unpaid parental leave if they have completed at least 12 months of continuous service with their employer.

Also ask about any conditions that may apply to paid leave. I know, for example, that some organisations require you to pay back any paid parental leave if you don't return to work or do come back but don't stay for at least six months. This is important because if you think you may not return to work then you'll have to budget to pay that back.

If you have unused annual leave or long service leave you may consider using it to help cover the costs while you're on leave.

## Extra help from the government

Remember, too, plenty of financial help is available from the government. Parental Leave Pay, which is fully government funded, is paid for a maximum period of 18 weeks at $812.45 a week before tax (the national minimum wage). It includes a continuous "Paid Parental Leave" period of up to 12 weeks (60 payable days) and 30 "Flexible Paid Parental Leave" days, which can be used on days that you aren't working and caring for your child. They must be used within two years of your child's birth or adoption.

To be eligible for paid parental leave you must have worked for at least 10 of the 13 months before the birth or adoption of your child for a minimum of 330 hours, around one day a week, in that 10 month period. You must have a taxable income of $156,647 or less in the financial year either before the date of birth or adoption, or the date you claim, whichever is earlier. (This income threshold is for the 2021-22 financial year.)

If you're not eligible for Parental Leave Pay you may be entitled to Family Tax Benefit Part A (see below) or you may be able to claim the Newborn Upfront Payment, which is a lump sum of $595, and the Newborn Supplement, which is an ongoing payment for up to 13 weeks. The amount of the Newborn Supplement depends on how many children you have and your family's income. The maximum you'll get for the first child is $1785.42 and for subsequent children the maximum is $596.05.

There's also Dad and Partner Pay. Eligible working dads and partners (including same-sex partners) get two weeks' leave paid at the national minimum wage rate ($812.45 a week). To be eligible for this scheme they can't be working or taking paid leave during their two-week DAP pay period. It's worth checking if you're entitled to Family Tax Benefit (FTB), which is split into Part A and Part B. The rate for Part A depends on your income and the

# Need to know

After the baby is born, don't forget to add your newborn to your Medicare card. And if you have private health insurance make sure you let your insurer know to add them to your policy.

ages and number of children in your care. It can be worth between $197.96 and $257.46 a fortnight per child. You may also get the FTB Part A annual supplement which can be up to $817.60 for each eligible child.

Family Tax Benefit Part B is for single parents and couples where the primary earner earns up to $104,432 a year. The maximum rate depends on the age of your youngest child. It is $168.28 a fortnight if your youngest child is 0 to 5 years and $117.46 a fortnight when your youngest is 5 to 18.

Head to servicesaustralia.gov.au for more details on eligibility criteria and payment rates. Figures are adjusted at least annually in line with inflation.

## Start getting ready for the changes

One of the best tips I have is to get used to living off one income in the lead-up to the due date. You can either save that money to use while you're on leave or use it towards paying off some debts.

If you have a mortgage, the repayments will probably be one of your biggest regular expenses, so paying extra will get you ahead, meaning you may be able to pay less while on leave. Not that I encourage that but it is an option if things are really tight.

If you think you'll have trouble keeping up with repayments, you can ask your lender if they have a parental option that lets you reduce or pause your repayments while on parental leave. Keep in mind that although your repayments may be on pause the interest isn't. It keeps compounding. Fees may also apply.

Now is also the time you'll probably be decluttering your house and getting ready for the impending arrival. Instead of tossing the stuff out for a council rubbish pick-up, try to sell what you can to fatten your wallet.

## Get your affairs in order

Yes, this means updating your will to reflect your new situation. And if you didn't have one before, you should definitely have one now. One of the nail-biting decisions you'll need to make is choosing a guardian to take care of your child and manage your assets in case you and your partner die. Think about who will be up to the task – for example, elderly family members may struggle. Also have a chat to them so it doesn't come as a complete surprise!

Make sure you also get a binding nomination for your super as well, as this won't be handled with the rest of your estate.

Insurance is another must – particularly life insurance for you and your partner. That way you can ensure your partner and child(ren) can take care of living costs and education expenses if the worst was to happen.

And don't forget to think ahead to your own financial future. Super isn't paid on parental leave payments so taking a break can mean your super will take a hit. There are tips in Chapter 8 ("Who's got spare cash to contribute to super?") to help you combat this.

## Going back to work

It might be three months, it might be 12 months or it might be two years but if you're planning to go back to work then another expense you will need to budget for is childcare – unless you're lucky enough to have family to look after your offspring when you're at work. Childcare fees can be as much as $200 a day in some areas, so going back to work won't be cheap.

You may be eligible for a Child Care Subsidy. If your family income is $72,466 or less, you may receive 85% of what you pay on childcare. Then between $72,466 and $177,465 your subsidy goes down by 1% for every $3000 of income your family earns, to 50% for the top amount. It keeps reducing the more your family earns. Families earning $356,756 or more will get nothing.

The Albanese government has pledged to increase the maximum subsidy rate to 90% for the first child in care. Also, all families earning under $530,000 a year will be eligible for the subsidy but at the time of writing this was not in place.

You can claim online through myGov but you'll need to link your Centrelink account. You'll need to provide details about how much you earn and the type of childcare that you're using.

Even if you don't intend to return to work in the short term, you should be careful not to make a decision that has a long-term effect on your career. Taking an extended break can limit your career options if you do want to go back eventually. Consider working part-time or upgrading your skills through further education or training. It's also a good idea to maintain your professional contacts as this will help you when you decide to re-enter the workforce.

#  Checklist

☐ *Come up with a budget of what your expenses are likely to be after you give birth.*

☐ *Try to cut back on your financial commitments.*

☐ *Don't take on anything new and focus on paying off your debts.*

☐ *Practise living on one income during the pregnancy.*

☐ *Find out whether you have any paid entitlements from your employer.*

☐ *Find out whether you are entitled to any government assistance.*

☐ *Make sure you have adequate life and income protection insurance in place.*

☐ *Update your will to ensure it reflects the changes in your situation.*

☐ *Think about your financial future and try to continue adding to super.*

☐ *Make sure you have childcare arrangements in place before returning to work.*

## LET'S GET REAL ...

They say kids are the best investment you'll ever make. While I'm yet to see a return on either of my children, the beauty of having two kids is that I've diversified, so whatever losses one incurs I'm hoping the gains of the other are greater. Jokes aside, I do love my children and am thankful for the day they came into my life. But, gee whiz, they cost a bomb. Like most first-time parents, I went all out with the first child. Probably not as bad as Cardi B, who reportedly bought her daughter a $US100,000 diamond necklace for her first birthday but you get the gist – nice clothes, nice birthday parties, nice things and so on. Come the second child and you're much wiser. Redirect the savings into an investment for them and they'll thank you when they're older.

As a parent you need to remind yourself that you don't have to spend a fortune to have a great time. It's the memories, not the material things. The best memory my son has isn't holidaying on some island with Mummy and Daddy, watching them drink margaritas by the pool but he does have fond memories of us riding our bikes alongside him to the local park. Him pushing me so hard on the swings and me begging him to stop. We laughed so much that day and it cost us nothing.

# CHAPTER

# 10

*Kids cost a bomb*

# If you only do one thing...

Start setting aside some money into a savings fund for your child from an early stage. No matter whether the cash is used for education, paying for braces at age 15 or to help buy a car when they turn 17, it's a fair bet that at some point you'll be glad you had savings to tap into. By starting early you'll get the benefit of compounding returns.

## AS A MOTHER OF TWO, I KNOW THAT CHILDREN ARE WONDERFUL, AN AWESOME SOURCE OF LOVE, LAUGHS AND PRIDE – AND THE BEST INVESTMENT YOU'LL EVER MAKE. BUT THEY DON'T COME CHEAP.

No matter whether you are a high-income earner or on a more modest wage, it pays to plan for the cost of kids. The blur of years from birth to adulthood will pass in the blink of an eye – and those first 18 years cover so much! We need to manage everything from maternity leave to sleep deprivation, paying for childcare, then school fees, organising pocket money and chores, juggling work with school pick-up times – and ensuring there are still funds in the kitty to enjoy a decent retirement. Is it a challenge? Yes. Can it be done? You bet!

## From prams to P-plates

In Chapter 9 ("Help, I'm pregnant"), I look at managing the costs of raising a baby. But don't think it all ends when your munchkin has graduated from nappies to fully fledged toilet training, or from childcare to kindergarten. For families, the outflow of cash keeps going – at least until your child turns 18, and possibly well beyond.

The cost of raising two children to age 18 can add up to hundreds of thousands for a typical middle-income family. Thankfully, this bill doesn't arrive in one hit. But every age brings a new range of expenses that you need to prepare for. Let's take a look at what you can expect at each of the main stages of childhood.

## Age five to 12 – primary school years

In seven short years from the age of five through to 12, your child will develop rapidly and there will be a range of costs that come with them growing.

Kids go through major growth spurts at this stage, so each change of season demands a completely new wardrobe (lucky them!). Their appetite gradually increases until those bite-size morsels they ate as toddlers have morphed into full-sized plates to be wolfed down – and that means a bigger grocery bill.

There are some costs you probably won't see coming. One mum of three I know found herself upgrading the family car from a basic sedan to a seven-seater – something she hadn't banked on doing when the kids were little. But as they grew, a bigger car was necessary to accommodate not just the kids, their bikes, skateboards and scooters – but their friends and all their friends' gear as well.

If you are buying a new car, better make it a fuel-efficient model because you're going to be doing a lot more driving. Once your little angel turns five, you're likely to find yourself chauffeuring him or her from dance class to swimming lessons, Saturday morning football or netball and, of course, picking up and dropping off friends who stay for sleepovers. (Trust me, your child's social life will eclipse your own.)

On the issue of social lives, one unexpected expense can be birthday parties. Forget fairy bread and pass the parcel. Kids parties are becoming bigger-than-Ben-Hur events with a price tag to match. Several years ago, Beyonce spent $US80,000 on a diamond-encrusted Barbie for her daughter's first birthday gift, then backed it up with that $US200,000 party. I still wonder if the doll suffered the fate of most Barbies – having her hair hacked short and texta smeared over her face. But the fact remains that mega stars aren't the only ones who lavish big bucks on their child's birthday parties.

Parents can feel under tremendous pressure to outdo other families to host the best ever birthday party. It can mean handing over hundreds, even thousands, of dollars for petting zoos, inflatable jumping castles and the must-have visit from a fairy or superhero. I tried to convince my then nine-year-old not to have a birthday party and even offered him $500 in exchange for a party. But, no … he wouldn't be in it.

If you can't afford a no-holds-barred event, think about what matters to your child. You don't need to spend a lot of money for kids to have a good time. If they love getting out and about, maybe hire a mini-van and take the birthday child and a bunch of mates to your nearest park, where they can let off some steam running around. It's got to be cheaper and better value than paying a small fortune for a clown to make balloon animals.

# Age 13 to 18 – secondary school

The teenage years can be especially expensive. One of the main costs is education, which I'll come to shortly. But the same basics apply – food, groceries, transport – only the bill gets bigger as children get older.

Clothing can become surprisingly expensive. By the time children hit high school, not only have they often outgrown children's sizes, they suddenly become acutely aware of the latest fashion trends. Those budget-friendly brands from the local department store no longer cut the mustard, and teens often turn up their noses at hand-me-downs. Instead, you're likely to come under plenty of pressure to spend up big on what your child deems "acceptable" clothing labels (read: the expensive ones). That's despite the reality that your growing teen will still be lucky to get a single season's wear from the clothes.

Your child may also join the burgeoning number of Aussie kids whose parents hand over upwards of $6000 to have their kids' smiles perfected by braces – a cost not covered by Medicare. And as they head towards the end of high school, teens reach milestones that can really hit the family budget hard. High school graduation outfits are just one example. One mum couldn't wait to go "formal" shopping with her daughter. She sensibly set a limit of $250, although after finding nothing suitable, the budget loosened up a little and the dress ended up costing over $500. That was just the beginning. The final bill nearly doubled, after shoes, jewellery, hair and make-up were added in.

If you've survived to this point, it pays to factor in the cost of teaching your children to drive. Along with professional driving lessons (allow from $70 an hour unless you have nerves of steel and plan to teach your children yourself), some families chip in to help their child buy a car.

Of course, these days kids are far more likely to remain at home after finishing school, so the expenses may keep rolling in.

# Live well on a budget — ways to save

The bottom line is that children not only cost a bomb, they get more expensive as they get older. One of the challenges families face is that the cost of raising children comes at a time when we face other major outgoings, such as paying off a home loan and maybe a car loan or two. This explains why in almost seven out of 10 families both parents work.

There is no single answer to meeting the costs of raising children. Sticking very carefully to a budget makes good sense. And often having children forces us to watch our spending more closely. There are, however, plenty of ways to save.

## Groceries

One of the best ways to save a bundle on food is to cook your own. Yes, it's easier said than done – especially if two parents work and everyone is time poor – but you'll pay a lot more for convenience foods and takeaways or home-delivery from local restaurants.

Meals don't have to be complex. A couple of steaks and veggies cooked on the barbecue can be ready in a few minutes. If you've got time to cook on weekends, try doubling quantities for something like pasta dishes and freeze half for mid-week dinners.

Meal planning can also help you save some cash. Constant trips to the corner store will mean paying a lot more than necessary for the basics. Aim for one big weekly supermarket shop (make a list so nothing is overlooked) or if you're super stretched for time shop online and have everything home-delivered.

## Hobbies and sports

There are lots of ways to save on extracurricular activities. Almost all organisations – from sport clubs to ballet schools, offer a discount if you register early and pay in full upfront. It almost always works out cheaper than paying by the week. If you're not sure how interested your child really is, ask for a trial before you commit to a series of expensive lessons.

If your child wants to learn a musical instrument, ask about lessons available through your school – visiting music tutors often charge way less than private ones. Rent an instrument or buy second-hand rather than investing in a new one. At least until you know whether or not they're going to keep it up.

It's worth looking into whether your state or territory government offers concessions or rebates for kids sport or creative activities.

## Holiday

Think back to what was memorable about your own childhood holidays – the time we share with our kids on vacation is often what makes a holiday special rather than how much money you spend. Camping trips are popular with families because they are super low cost. Borrow some gear from friends or rent equipment to try it out. If the idea of pitching a tent fills you with dread, rent a cabin at a beachside camping ground.

Consider booking an apartment instead of a hotel. That way you can prepare a lot of your meals yourself and don't have to spend a fortune eating out three times a day.

Or for low-cost accommodation with a twist, you could try house swapping. This is where two families, anywhere in the world, swap homes for a given period. In most cases, once you pay a joining fee, your accommodation is free.

## Mobile plans

One of the unforeseen costs of having children, especially as they get older, is the additional expense of staying digitally connected.

It's not unusual to see primary school children equipped with the latest iPhone. Lucky for them is all I can say, because somebody else is clearly funding that plan for them. The good news is that there are plenty of kid-friendly plans, so the days of kids racking up $1000 mobile bills should be long behind us, assuming you stick to plans with automatic data top-ups disabled. If you opt for a prepaid plan and they hit their data limit before their expiry period they

# Need to know

*Sometimes you just need to explain to your kids that you can't afford something. Overcoming the need to "keep up with the Joneses" is a simple way to avoid getting deep in debt to pay for things that aren't essential to raising happy, healthy kids. It also means you're free to enjoy your children rather than poring over a pile of bills that you'll struggle to pay.*

will just have to live without it! Of course, they can recharge early or they may be able to add extra data (for a fee). You may also be able to find a postpaid plan that won't hit them with excess data charges. When they reach their data limit they will reduce the data speed.

Be sure to give the smaller carriers a chance because they use the same networks as the big ones, so you may be able to get the same coverage for a fraction of the price.

If you're just about to set up your kid with their first phone, be sure to check your drawers for any old phones or buy second-hand.

Once your child is old enough to get a part-time job, be sure to make them responsible for at least part of the plan.

## Toys

A low-cost way to give young children aged up to five access to a wide variety of toys is through play groups. These are informal weekly gatherings of children and parents or carers, often held in places like community halls. It costs next to nothing to attend each week and the money raised is used to fund new toys, and art and craft activities.

For older children, don't go overboard with toys – they really don't need that many. But do buy quality items so that they last for a while. Arrange to swap toys with friends instead of buying new all the time – and remember, the toys your child will enjoy most are the ones that let you join in. A football is not much fun on your own but it can make for a great afternoon if Mum or Dad are happy to have a game in the backyard.

# MANAGING THE COSTS OF EDUCATION

*When you see parents crying as their child totters off in a one-size-too-big uniform on their first day at "big" school, there's every chance that what you're seeing are tears of relief as they say goodbye to exorbitant childcare fees. But as I mentioned earlier, one of the biggest costs of raising kids is giving them an education.*

If you send your kids to the local public school, the switch from paid childcare to a low-cost education system can seem like a money-saving moment. Don't be fooled, though. Even the "free" public system can come with a solid price tag. That's because schooling almost always costs more than you expect and it pays to allow for much more than basic tuition fees.

Planning for your child's education is easier when you break down the process into three steps: work out how much it's likely to cost; look at your budget to know what you can realistically afford to pay; and consider how you will save or invest money towards your child's education.

## What's it going to cost?

Public schools certainly sit at the most affordable end of the spectrum but you'll still be asked to pay for uniforms, textbooks, excursions and, these days, digital devices such as laptops or tablets. According to education fund provider Futurity Investment Group, educating your child through the public system in major cities can cost a total of $83,869 from K to 12. This cost rises to $143,944 for the Catholic system or as much as $349,404 for the independent private school sector. For the parents paying for it all, it gives new meaning to the term "capital punishment".

The sheer scale of these costs makes it critical to be realistic about which school you can comfortably afford to send your child to. Head back to your budget to know what you can afford to pay.

## Can you get financial support?

If you'd like to send your child to a private school but can't handle the cost, think about applying for a scholarship. Almost all independent schools offer a range of scholarships that can see fees get slashed to almost nothing. Not a bad deal if you can get it.

Scholarships are usually awarded based on exam results, and they can be set by individual schools or the Australian Council of Education Research (ACER). For more details, contact the school of your choice or head to acer.org/scholarship.

If your child fails to win a scholarship, consider a bursary. These are usually awarded to children who are academically strong but whose family income doesn't stretch to meeting school fees.

There are also a number of subsidies and rebates available from state and territory governments that may help with some school costs. You may have to meet certain conditions to be eligible but it's worth exploring what's on offer.

## Where will you save?

The type of investment you use to save for school costs matters – but what also matters is whose name the investments will be held in, because part of your ongoing returns will be lost to tax. Avoid the urge to put savings in your child's name because kids face very high tax rates on investment income.

A savings account may seem like a good way to save but the catch is that private school fees generally rise by more than inflation so your money needs to keep pace by earning more than the low return you'll get on cash savings.

Investment bonds, also known as insurance bonds, are an option worth considering because you'll get the benefit of tax savings. They work like a managed fund but are a tax-paid investment. You hand your money over to the fund manager to invest on your behalf, your fund deals with the tax, paying a rate of 30%, which could be lower than your personal tax rate. Provided you leave the fund in place for 10 years, any withdrawals later on are tax free.

It is possible to make additional contributions to insurance bonds but these are capped by the 125% rule. It means that for second and subsequent years of holding the bond, additional contributions must be less than 125% of the previous year's investment. So if your initial investment is, say, $4000 the maximum that can be contributed in the second year is $5000. This is inflexible but the upside is that you don't have to use the money exclusively to pay for education. The funds saved can be used for a family holiday if, for example, your child bails out of the private system and goes into the more affordable public system.

As the table on page 131 shows, you'll need to save from about $260 to $1700 a month (depending on your choice of school), if you use insurance bonds.

An alternative is education bonds offered by the likes of Futurity Investment Group and Australian Unity. They work in a very similar way to investment bonds though they can be less flexible. You may only be paid the returns your investment earns when your child enters university, which some kids will choose not to do. Bottom line, read the fine print carefully.

As we saw in Chapter 7 ("I'm ready to start investing"), exchange traded funds (ETFs) are a low-cost type of investment, and while the brokerage cost can add up, it's possible to minimise this expense by only investing when you have a reasonable sum of cash to tip into the fund. Using ETFs or even a low-cost unlisted managed fund, you'll need from about $271 up to $1211 a month to cover school costs.

Here's a third option to consider: using your home loan. It can be done by depositing savings into an offset account or making extra repayments into your loan and redrawing cash when it's needed for education expenses.

As a guide, a family using their home loan to pay for a government school education would need to set aside $300 each month, rising to $1345 for the private system – more than for either insurance bonds, ETFs or unlisted funds. That's because home loan rates are so low. The other drawback is that this method calls for plenty of discipline to keep making extra repayments and resist dipping into your mortgage to pay for other things.

The main point is that not all families can afford private schools – and that shouldn't be an issue as the public system provides a high-quality education. But if your heart is set on the private system, unless you're a high-income earner it makes a lot of sense to invest for the costs from an early stage, so that your returns do at least part of the work of helping to foot the bill.

If you're not sure how much you should be saving for education costs, moneysmart.gov.au has a savings goal calculator that lets you see how much you need to save regularly to meet a particular target.

# MONTHLY INVESTMENT REQUIRED TO FUND DIFFERENT EDUCATION OPTIONS

| INVESTMENT OPTION[1] | MONTHLY INVESTMENT CONTRIBUTION REQUIRED TO COVER EDUCATION COSTS | | |
|---|---|---|---|
| | Private system – total education costs from K to 12 of $349,404[2] | Catholic system – total education costs from K to 12 of $143,944[2] | Government system – total education costs from K to 12 of $83,869[2] |
| Investment bond[3] | $1280 | $456 | $286 |
| Exchange traded fund/unlisted managed fund[4] | $1211 | $428 | $271 |
| Pay extra into home loan[6] | $1345 | $480 | $300 |

1: Assumes savings rise by 2.15% annually over a 19-year period.

2: Total education costs for a child born in 2022, commencing kindergarten in 2027 and completing Year 12 in 2040.

3: Assumes earnings of 6.0%pa and MER of 1.30%.

4: Assumes focus on Australian shares, with earnings of 6.50%pa and MER of 0.50%.

5: Assumes 3.5%pa interesr rate.

Table provides indicative figures only and should not be regarded as applying to all families or be taken as financial advice.

*Source: Apt Wealth Partners (aptwealth.com.au)*

# WHEN DOES IT ALL END?

As our children grow from toddlers to teens, parents face a common dilemma. Let me share a story with you to explain what I mean.

Not so long ago I came across a news article about a luckless New York couple who had taken their 30-year-old son to court in a last-ditch effort to boot him out of home, where he was enjoying a rent-free ride. It's easy to think "only in America" but here in Australia we're tending to stay at home for longer too.

At the other end of the spectrum, I have a friend whose teenage kids regularly stir their mum with warnings of, "You better be nice to us because we'll be paying for your nursing home".

There are two extremes here that as parents we have to deal with – the need to raise our children to become financially independent adults balanced with the need to manage our own financial wellbeing so that we're not dependent on our children later in life.

Like so many aspects of parenting, this can be a fine line. Once your child is earning decent money, you may want to address the issue of charging board. Continually providing a free ride when your kids are earning an independent income can encourage an unrealistic view of how the world works. Forking out for your adult children can also soak up your own money at a time when you should focus more on planning for retirement.

How you deal with board is a very personal issue. You might use the board to help you stretch your money further. Another option is to put the money away in a savings account and give it back to your child to use towards a house deposit when they are ready to get onto the property ladder.

When you feel the time is right, try broaching the subject of board and contributing to household bills with tact. None of us enjoys discovering that we're suddenly expected to fork out cash on a regular basis, but be firm. However much you choose to charge, board should be paid regularly. This sends a strong message that bills need to be paid on time, and they need to be paid first – before money is spent on non-essentials. That's one of the basics of good money management, and it's a lesson we should pass on to our kids.

# Checklist

☐ *Look for ways to cut costs without compromising your kids. Birthday parties, for instance, don't have to involve a big spend to be a big success.*

☐ *Plan for how you will manage school costs, especially if you opt for the private system.*

☐ *Know the likely cost and how much you can afford to regularly save, then choose an investment to grow your education savings.*

☐ *Don't be afraid to charge your children board as they move into adulthood — learning to pay their way is a stepping stone to adulthood.*

## LET'S GET REAL ...

Will my kids ever leave home? Surely, I can't be the only parent who has ever asked this question? To be fair, my 21-year-old has kinda moved out as she is studying in Canberra but given I'm still subsidising her expenses I'm not sure if it really counts. As for my 16-year-old, I don't think he has any plans of moving out of home ever. We all want our kids to be able to stand on their own two feet financially and I think that comes down to how much of an effort you've put into their money skills. I strongly believe money lessons are learnt, not taught. Take the spending bender that my son went on a few years ago. Home alone, he took it upon himself to dabble in some virtual currency. Not cryptocurrency – I may have forgiven him if it had been that – but virtual currency within a game called Fortnite. Within a couple of hours, he converted $150 worth of Xbox gift cards (real dollars) into V-Bucks. His response when he got caught? "It's not that bad – it's not my money anyway." His reaction after I explained the lesson here – about valuing money whether you've earned it or had a windfall – was pure regret and remorse. "I won't ever do that again!" Lesson learnt!

# CHAPTER

# 11

Will my kids ever
leave home?

# If you only do one thing...

Get them saving. It might start with coins in a money box but as soon as they are school age, open a bank account. It doesn't matter if it's not the best rate. Kids' accounts aren't about becoming millionaires; it's just about teaching them how to save.

## RAISING KIDS IS REWARDING BUT IT BRINGS PLENTY OF RESPONSIBILITY.

In just 18 years, you will have guided your child through toilet training (thank goodness those days are over!) and tying shoelaces to driving a car.

So it can seem like a big ask to also teach your kids good money habits, but it's a case of "learn now or pay later", which translates to: if your kids don't learn they may never move out!

Research shows that the way we handle our finances as an adult is strongly influenced by our childhood experiences with money. The reality is that we teach our children plenty about the world just through our own behaviour. A study by Cambridge University found that children's basic attitudes to money are formed by age seven. Scary, huh? It happens because they closely watch and listen to their parents, soaking up plenty of information about money, how it should be handled and its impact – good and bad – on our lives. Psychologists call it "behavioural shaping" and it can have a lasting impact.

The trick is not to stress over what you're saying about money in front of the kids. Sure, waving the credit statement at your other half while you yell, "You spent how much on those new golf clubs?", won't help. It's more about having conversations that encourage your kids to have a positive attitude towards money.

The money conversations around our house have covered everything from the latest electricity bills (my son has been known to tell guests to switch off the bathroom lights), to credit cards versus debit cards, to super (relevant when my daughter got her first job), to the cost of their education.

Something as simple as chatting about your grocery budget while you're out shopping or helping them plan for the next family holiday can be a great way to engage children.

One of the best savings tools I gave my children when they were younger was slapping their name on a tomato paste jar and calling it the 52-week challenge. You start by putting away just $1 in the first week, and then gradually increase the amount by $1 a week throughout the year. So you save $2 in week two building up to $52. If you complete the challenge, you'll have saved $1378.

The deal was that I would match the savings for the child who met the challenge. Thankfully, only one out of the two managed to complete it. The younger one found it a little too hard to come up with the bigger dollars needed.

# Digital world

We live in a digital world, which can make things a little tougher. Many of your kids' purchases will be "invisible". One of my son's first purchases was an app on my phone. As for my daughter, the biggest mistake I made was allowing her to download Uber onto her phone but link it to my credit card. She was nearly 18 and in no rush to get her licence – and why would she be when she has access to "free" rides. (Even though I put an end to that, almost four years later she is still no closer to getting her licence.) Then there are things like buy now pay later schemes. Explain how these services work and how they can encourage you to spend more without you realising.

# Valuable lessons

Where do you start? I remember someone once saying that when your child first shows an interest in books, you don't start by giving them *War and Peace*, and it's the same with money. Here are some age-appropriate tips:

## PRESCHOOLERS (3-5 YEARS)

• Play shop using pretend money so they understand the concept of trading money for goods.

• Explain where money comes from – for example, you are paid for working.

• Describe what $2 or $5 actually buys.

• Let them practise putting away their money in a piggy bank.

## AGES 6-9

• Set up a savings account specifically for them. Explain that they'll be paid extra money (interest) by having their money in an account.

• Talk to your children about the difference between needs and wants, and how they can budget their money based on these.

• Teach kids to compare prices when at the shops.

• Encourage them to set savings goals and explain how long it will take to achieve them. If they want a toy worth $25, explain that if they save $1 a week it will take 25 weeks. Consider using a chart so they can see their progress.

• You might offer to match their savings to give them an extra incentive to save. For every dollar they save you might opt to match it with 50c or even $1.

• Help them understand the importance of not making impulse purchases. If they spot something they want to buy, encourage them to wait a few days before making the purchase even if they have the money.

• Teach them about the importance of giving to help those in need. You might start with giving away toys they no longer play with before progressing to money.

• If you're buying an app on a tablet, don't just put in the password and let them have it. Explain that it is real money and give them an idea of what that could get them in the "real" world. You might even ask them to pay for it with their pocket money.

## AGES 10-15

• Show them what bills look like and how you plan to pay them.

• They may not be able to get a "proper" job but encourage them to find ways to make some extra cash, like walking the dog or washing the car.

• Explain the concept of credit and borrowing money. If they want to buy something they can't afford, consider lending them money and getting them to pay you back. You can even set out a repayment schedule.

• Teach the basics of the sharemarket. You can pretend to invest in companies and then watch how they perform.

• Get them to put their own money towards an iTunes voucher. They will then spend their own money for apps or songs. This will make them think twice before buying something.

## 16-PLUS

• Encourage them to get a casual job.

• If they are earning money, make them responsible (or at least partly) for some of the bills you may have been taking care of for them. For example, maybe they need to pay for their own mobile usage or for buying gifts for friends.

• Once they have built up some savings, they can begin to invest. You might start by investing in an ETF or buying a small parcel of shares in a company they have heard of. Be careful about whose name you invest in as there could be tax implications.

• Talk to them about "buy now and pay later" schemes. Explain how they work and encourage them to do the opposite and save for what they want.

# Pocket money is a great tool

Paying pocket money is another practical step. Personally I'm not a big fan of paying them just for the sake of it. Setting some age-suitable chores can help them learn that money has to be earned. For example, my husband and I sat down with each child and put together a contract outlining what was expected in return for payment. If they completed the list they got paid.

As for how much to give them, it comes down to what you'd like to achieve. If you want them to learn about budgeting and have them cover some costs, then you'll need to make sure you're paying them enough to cover their expenses. If it's purely to teach them the art of saving, the amount doesn't really matter.

Talk about different ways they can use the money. Some can be set aside for treats but you should encourage your children to start saving and even to put away some money for charity.

There are even a number of apps that can help. For example, Spriggy, FLX and ZAAP allow parents to allocate money to their children's prepaid Visa card. They can set savings goals and they (and you) can see their transactions in the app. Fees apply though and no interest will be paid.

If you don't want them to have a prepaid card then you might prefer something like Chores & Allowance Bot. There's no "real" money but you can set tasks and track how much money they have earned. When they want to spend any you'll have to give it to them and "withdraw" the amount from their balance.

# Get them their own account

If you really want to encourage saving, open a savings account just for them and encourage them to put away some money each month. A good account has zero fees and a decent rate of interest.

Most kids accounts are set up as "bonus saver" accounts, which means they'll get extra interest if they meet certain conditions, such as depositing a minimum amount each month or making limited withdrawals. Just make sure you and your child understand any conditions attached to the account and that you're confident they can meet them.

Some cash from birthday and Christmas money from family can go into the savings pool. My book *The Great $20 Adventure* is a fun way to help young children learn how to make money decisions.

# Checklist

- ☐ *Be open about money – it's not a dirty word.*
- ☐ *Include your children in conversations about household bills and savings goals.*
- ☐ *Explain simple concepts: for example, people get money by working – it doesn't come from a machine in the wall. Then, as they get older, you can teach them about more complex issues.*
- ☐ *Encourage them to save from a young age.*
- ☐ *Use pocket money as a tool to teach them about the value of money, budgeting and saving for what they want.*
- ☐ *Open a bank account just for them.*
- ☐ *When they are older, help them to graduate from saving to investing.*

# LET'S GET REAL ...

Quite some time ago I was at a property expo. *Money* magazine, which I edited at the time, would often be asked to participate in such events, where we would set up a stand and I'd have the honour of talking to property buyers about mortgages, finding the best deals and so on. After the seminar, people would come to the stand and ask all sorts of questions. It was the perfect opportunity to meet readers and I'd often walk away with some great story ideas from all the chit-chat.

Surprisingly, people at expos are only too happy to reveal their darkest and deepest money secrets. I've heard just about everything. Like the woman who racked up $60,000 on her credit card, sent the statements to a private PO box and wondered if her husband would find out because they were applying for a home loan. Or the lady who had to start all over again at the age of 40 and didn't even know what bank her accounts were with. Without any warning she came up to me and blurted out: "He left me for his secretary." It had happened 10 years earlier and since then she had reskilled herself, got a job while raising her son and was now at the expo planning to buy her first home. She was inspirational! I don't think she coined the saying "a man is not a plan" but it was the first time I'd heard it. I loved it then and I still love it now.

# CHAPTER

# 12

## The bastard left me for somebody younger

# If you only do one thing...

Get a decent lawyer and do it early. Family law is complex and you need to know where you stand. Professional advice is especially important for your property settlement, which can have an enormous impact on your future.

## HE'S FOUND SOMEONE ELSE, ANNOUNCED HE'S LEAVING, PACKED HIS BAGS AND GONE. WHAT A BASTARD!

Whether your partner left you for a younger woman (or man), or whether after 20 years of marriage you two woke up one morning and asked yourselves "What do we have in common?", divorce happens.

What matters now is that you take control of your situation. The end of a long-term relationship is tough and along with emotional pain there will be financial repercussions. Becoming single may not be what you expected or wanted but you need to do whatever it takes to secure your future financial wellbeing.

### Speak to your lawyer

One thing you can do right now is to speak to a lawyer, preferably a family law specialist, to know where you stand. Marriage is a legal arrangement and undoing it can be complex. There are three main issues to sort out:

• *Parenting arrangements* – how you will share the care of your children.

• *Child support payments* – who will pay what towards the cost of raising your children.

• *Your property settlement* – how your assets will be split up.

By law you can't use the same solicitor as your former spouse or partner. If your soon-to-be ex has already engaged the services of your regular family solicitor, you'll need to find someone else.

Your lawyer can give you a preliminary idea of how your property settlement and child custody arrangements may pan out. Before you head into the meeting, make a list of questions to ask, including how you'll be billed for legal services. The fee metre starts ticking the minute you're across the desk from counsel and making good use of face-to-face time helps keep the cost down.

### Reset your budget

After separation or divorce, women typically see their household income drop significantly. That makes learning to live on less an absolute must, especially in the early days following separation. Until your property settlement and child support are worked out, you may be unclear about where you stand financially. Focus on what you can control right now by scaling back.

Accept that things are different and reset your budget for your new life – even if it is only for a short while, until things between you and your ex are sorted out. Head to Chapter 1 ("How can she afford that?") for tips on budgeting.

## Be prepared to re-enter the workforce

If you've been a homemaker, it pays to start looking for work or undertake some training to get back into the workforce from an early stage. You're going to need that income to support yourself.

Forget notions of taking your ex "to the cleaners" for spousal maintenance. We've all come across stories about Hollywood stars who pay tens of thousands in "alimony" but for ordinary Australians the situation isn't so lucrative.

Under Australian family law, your ex may only have to pay spousal maintenance (as distinct from child support) if you're unable to adequately support yourself and they can reasonably afford to pay it. The bottom line is that now is the time to invest in yourself.

If you're short on cash right now, head to Chapter 13 ("I want to leave him but can't afford to") for the different types of government support available.

## Revenge – don't go there

You may be itching to take the gardening shears to your ex's tailor-made suits, or to give away his prized 10-year-old malt whiskey collection but resist the urge. Taking the wrecking ball to your ex's belongings could land you in trouble. One woman gifted her cheating ex-husband's entire wine collection to the neighbours. Another took an axe to her ex's expensive desk. Yes, it must have felt pretty darn good at the time but all you will be doing is lowering the value of the assets to be shared between you.

Australia's divorce system works on a "no fault" basis. As far as the courts are concerned, it doesn't matter that your ex ran off with a woman 20 years his junior after you have given him four gorgeous children and sacrificed your career. What the Family Court will consider is what is "fair and reasonable". The challenge is that its definition of "fair" may not match your own.

From a legal perspective, the property that will be considered for your settlement covers just about everything that you own either individually or together – as well as your individual and combined debts. It's all tossed into the marital pool to be divided up.

On the plus side, it doesn't matter if you've been a homemaker rather than a breadwinner. This is still regarded as a valid contribution to the household and shouldn't have a negative impact on your share of the settlement. We'll come back to the property settlement shortly.

## Try to work things out between yourselves

No matter how you feel towards your ex, try to work out child custody and property issues without heading off to do battle in court. A legal battle can mean spending tens of thousands, even hundreds of thousands of dollars in court costs and lawyers' fees, and you may not get the outcome you wanted.

If you and your ex can't agree on things, consider mediation. You may have to pay for the service but it will still be cheaper than going to court. Contact the Family Relationship Advice Line 1800 050 321 for more information on mediation.

## Child support – compare options

One of the biggest decisions you and your ex need to make is how much time your kids will spend with each of you. This really is something you need to work out at an early stage – for your children's sake if nothing else. But it also has a financial impact as your parenting arrangements will shape how much child support you're entitled to.

Family law encourages both parents to have an equal say in the raising of their children. However, that doesn't have to mean equal time spent with both, and the reality is that women often end up doing most of the child raising. You're going to need money to do this, and that makes child support essential.

How much you receive will normally depend on the income you each earn, the number of children and their ages, and how much time the children spend with you both. For the record, it is nights spent with each parent that count, not just daytime hours. Think this through carefully and speak to your lawyer because the agreement you make today may be in place until your kids turn 18.

You and your ex can come up with your own "parenting plan" as distinct from legally enforceable "parenting orders", which are determined by the courts. Your ex is entitled to make "in kind" payments, such as paying the kids' school fees directly to their school, rather than handing all the cash to you.

An alternative to a private agreement is to have child support determined by Services Australia. The website (servicesaustralia.gov.au) features a child support calculator that estimates how much you'll receive under its assessment. Even if you plan to make a private agreement, it's worth a look at the calculator to see how the numbers compare.

There are pros and cons when going through Services Australia. On the plus side, you won't have to deal with your ex. This can be incredibly valuable if he digs in his heels about paying child support (which isn't uncommon), or if he is likely to refuse to pay up. Services Australia has the power to contact your ex's employer and issue a garnishee notice, meaning his boss is directed to withhold child support from his wages.

The downside of using Services Australia is that child support hinges heavily on current income. If your ex loses his job or his income falls dramatically, you can be left with next to nothing in child support. By contrast, a private agreement may set a fixed monthly payment that holds no matter how much your ex earns. If you use Services Australia to work out child support, be prepared to live with its decision.

## Your children may want to see their other parent too

It can be a real thorn in your side to see your children totter off with your ex, knowing they will be spending time with her, too. However, it's important to hear out your children and consider what they want. Research by the Australian Institute of Family Studies found 76% of children from separated families wanted their parents to listen more to their views when they were working out living arrangements. It's one of the tougher aspects but it's something you need to come to terms with.

## Sort out the property issue, then move on

There's no telling exactly what your share of the property settlement will look like, but one thing is sure – while you need to have been separated for at least 12 months before you can apply for a formal divorce, you can, and sometimes should, get your property settlement (known as a binding financial agreement) sorted out much earlier.

Until your property settlement is worked out, you and your ex continue to have a financial relationship. That may sound warm and fuzzy but it's not.

# Need to know

*Either party can draw money from offset or redraw accounts on your mortgage, and primary cardholders are responsible for the debt of additional cardholders. If your partner leaves you, be sure to put all your accounts in lockdown to stop debt leakage.*

In practical terms it means either of you can make a claim on your ex's assets right up until the date your property settlement is finalised. That's because the pool of assets to be divided is based on the date of settlement.

This can work in your favour. In one case, a divorcing couple had almost zero assets when they separated. Eighteen months later the ex-husband won $5 million in the lottery and his former wife was awarded a stake in the winnings as part of the property settlement. Delaying tactics can work against you, though. If you decide to buy a home of your own after separating, your new place could go into the pool of marital assets to be divvied up.

The upshot is that it can be worth getting onto your property settlement sooner rather than later. That doesn't mean you should commit to an agreement immediately after separating just to get it over and done with. Your property settlement is set in cement, so think it through, don't sign anything until you've spoken to your lawyer and don't sell yourself short.

## The family home — do you really need it?

The family home can seem like a source of stability for you and your children but take off the rose-coloured glasses for a minute. Think long and hard about whether your home is the jewel in the crown of a property settlement or if it will be a financial millstone. Sure, you may be awarded the home but what about the mortgage? Consider whether you will need to take out a home loan in your own name to hang onto the place. Unless you have a good job with a reliable income, it could be a struggle. Selling up, paying off what's left on the home loan and splitting the remainder can let you move on and start afresh.

## Think ahead — don't give super away

As a newly separated woman, the struggle for day-to-day cash can be very real. That shouldn't mean you turn your back on a chunk of your ex's superannuation. It's money you can't access now but it could be a financial lifeline later.

Women typically have much less in super than men but we need it more as we tend to live longer. So when your combined super savings go into the pot of assets to be divided, don't be left shortchanged. Keep one eye on the future.

# Checklist

☐ *Speak to a lawyer so you know where you stand.*

☐ *Reset your budget. It can be fine-tuned later when child support and your property settlement are finalised.*

☐ *Invest in yourself. If you've been a homemaker you may need to retrain or upskill.*

☐ *You may need to switch from a part-time to a full-time role to get more money in.*

☐ *Divorce may take 12 months but sort out your property settlement ASAP. Try to work out any arrangements with your ex rather than heading to court. You'll save a fortune in legal fees.*

☐ *Look forwards not backwards.*

## LET'S GET REAL ...

I can't imagine what it would be like to be stuck in a relationship because of money, or lack of it. However, this open letter that was posted anonymously on the internet gave me a very raw insight into how painful it must be. She wrote:

*Writing this is probably the hardest thing I've ever done, because it means admitting to myself that I really am staying in a relationship for financial reasons. But I am no longer in love with him, I no longer want to be touched by him, and I no longer have dreams of spending my life with him ... I only hope I get back on my feet soon, so that I can take us both out of this purgatory.*

Whenever I'm dealing with a financial challenge I know if I do nothing, nothing will happen. Some decisions aren't easy and there is definitely discomfort in any transition, this is certainly one of them. Know that there are some things you can do and there is help for those that you can't.

# CHAPTER

# 13

## I want to leave him but I can't afford to

# If you only do one thing...

*As long as you think you can't afford to leave, you won't! You need to figure it out. Create a list of all your expenses as if you were living on your own. This will give you an idea of how much you need to earn to support yourself and any children. Remember that child custody and property settlement could support some of these expenses.*

## FOR SOME WOMEN, IT'S A FEELING THAT BUILDS OVER TIME. FOR OTHERS, IT COMES LIKE A BOLT OUT OF THE BLUE.

I'm talking about the realisation that you're unhappy in a relationship and you want out. But what if you don't have the financial means to walk away?

Few situations are worse than living with a partner you desperately want to leave but can't afford to. There are solutions, although for your own financial wellbeing it's worth planning your exit. And in case you're wondering, your ability to claim a share in the family home or any other assets built up by you and your partner should not be impacted by your decision to walk out of the relationship.

### Develop a plan of action

The first thing you need is an action plan. This doesn't have to be in writing. If your partner is likely to become suspicious that you're thinking of leaving, just keep the plan in your head. But do think carefully about how you'll manage financially, where you're going to live and how you will pay for everything.

You really need to take a good, hard look at your expenses and what you will need to pay for when you're on your own. That means groceries, gas and electricity, petrol, kids' activities, etc. Download a budgeting app to help work out the costs.

The biggest expense you'll probably need to factor in is accommodation. If you think you will stay in the family home and ask your partner to leave, then you'll need to factor in mortgage payments. If that's not an option then you may need to rent. Start looking at rental properties in your area to get an idea of how much you can expect to pay so that you can factor that in. There are organisations that can help you find temporary accommodation if you do need to leave in a hurry. Contact 1800RESPECT as a starting point.

### Build a f***-off fund

Fear of financial hardship is one of the most common reasons women stay in an unhappy relationship. And, yes, concerns about how you'll pay for basics like rent or groceries are very real, especially if children are involved. So start taking steps from an early stage to make the move easier.

If you don't have a bank account in your own name, open one as soon as possible. It's not just about having somewhere to stash away survival funds. Having a bank account of your own lets you build your personal financial identity – something that will be needed if you want to apply for a loan at some stage. Having your own account is also essential if you plan to receive government support payments – be it JobSeeker Payment if you're looking for work or Family Tax Benefit if you're raising kids.

If you already have a separate account in your name, good for you – be sure to change your PIN and online passwords.

Once your account is up and running, use it to build a personal f\*\*\*-off fund. Think of it as a financial safety net that's your ticket to freedom.

## Where will the money come from?

Yes, it can be hard to stash cash away but having even a small amount set aside will help to cover essentials like rent, utilities, food and transport until you're on your feet. Take a look at Chapter 2 ("How much should I be saving?") for simple hacks to grow savings using loose change.

Or get an extra $20 out each time you pay for groceries by card – it may not show up on your bank statement as an extra transaction. A slow but steady approach may be your best bet if you're worried that your other half will get suspicious about large sums of money going missing.

If you're not working and don't have any income, then you will need to look for ways to make some extra money to stay afloat until any settlement is finalised. Consider selling any unwanted items laying around the house to boost your kitty.

If finding a full-time job isn't an option, then look for ways to make extra money when you can. Make the most of any special talents you have. If you play an instrument or speak a second language you might be able to get work as a tutor.

If there's something you are interested in doing but don't have all the necessary skills, it may be worth doing a course that will give you valuable qualifications. For instance, if you love make-up find a local college where you can learn the skills and then hire yourself out to do make-up for weddings and parties.

Other options to make extra include babysitting, dog walking, taking on ironing jobs and becoming a personal grocery shopper. Also take a look at Chapter 1 ("How can she afford that?") for ways you can make money.

## You might be eligible for crisis cash

For a lot of women, getting by financially after they end a relationship can mean tapping into every available resource, in the early days at least. So it's worth knowing the different options you can access.

If you've experienced a family or domestic violence incident and are already receiving payments from Services Australia, a one-off "crisis" payment may be available. It's usually equal to one week's worth of any payment you're already receiving from Services Australia, so the exact amount will depend on the type of income support you're eligible for.

If you have not claimed any payments in the past, you may be eligible for a special benefit payment. To get this you must be ineligible for any other income support payment and in financial hardship.

Charities such as the Salvos (phone 1300 371 288) may also provide emergency financial assistance.

Longer term, a variety of income support payments are available that can tide you over if you're looking for work or studying or just need a bit of extra income to raise your kids. Your household income will change once you head out on your own, so even if you haven't been eligible for these types of payments in the past, now's the time for a second look.

It's worth calling the Services Australia support line (132 850) to find out where you stand. If possible, make an appointment to speak with a customer service officer face to face. It can be a lot easier to state your case in person rather than wading through the inevitable mountain of paperwork that's needed to receive payments. It can take several weeks for any support payments to come through, so make this a priority.

## Avoid taking on high interest debt

No matter how short of funds you are, resist the temptation to whack everything on the credit card or visit a payday lender. Now is not the time to start loading yourself up with debt. High fees and interest charges could put a real strain on your cash situation, potentially making it even harder for you to build a new life for yourself.

If you're in urgent need of funds, a better alternative is NILS – the No Interest Loan Scheme, which is available for low-income families. The loans are provided by hundreds of community organisations around Australia, with sums of up to $2000 available to pay for essential goods and services. Loans are interest-free and repayments are set at an affordable amount over a set period. To be eligible you'll need a health care or pension card or you have to be earning less than $70,000 a year (gross). Check out nils.com.au.

## Talk to a lawyer

It makes sense to get legal advice, preferably before you mention to your partner that you want to end the relationship. This way you have an idea of how to handle the situation if your partner becomes spiteful. Legal advice is especially helpful if you're worried about your partner pulling stunts like trying to hide assets or burying you in an expensive custody dispute.

Your solicitor can explain some of the big issues, including how your child custody and property settlement may work out. Your legal counsel may also explain the documents you're going to need as part of your separation (more on this later) or advise you to take photographs of your home to confirm the state of the residence at the time you leave.

A number of community legal centres and Legal Aid agencies offer free advice. Try doing an online search for women's legal services in your state or territory. Many will provide urgent advice over the phone.

## Gather records

Where possible, pull together a personal file of key documents that you're going to need for your new life. It can be a lot easier to do this when you're still in the relationship with access to everything in your home. It will also save you the cost and hassle of trying to chase down or replace paperwork later on.

Originals are best but if that's not possible get copies of birth certificates for yourself and your children, citizenship certificates or passports, your tax file number, and copies of bank statements, loan statements and super statements. These may all be needed for your property settlement. Check out Chapter 12 ("The bastard left me for somebody younger") for more info on the next steps.

# Need to know

If you're experiencing domestic abuse and need help, 1800**RESPECT** can provide information on support options available near you. You can call them on 1800 732 732 or chat online at 1800respect.org.au. You could also download the Daisy app which provides information about support services in your local area.

# Protect yourself financially

Your first priority may be to split from your partner but once you have left the relationship, act fast to protect your financial identity. Together with a good credit score, this will help you get re-established.

Your ex could dish up some dirty tricks like cleaning out a bank account held jointly in your names or accessing funds in your mortgage offset or redraw account. So get in touch with your bank and explain the situation. Request that any withdrawals or transfers can only be made if both you and your ex sign for the transaction.

On the flipside, don't be tempted to go on a "stuff you" spending spree with the money held in a joint account. The funds will form part of your property settlement regardless of who earnt the money. Any funds you withdraw and spend today could be deducted from your share of the property settlement when it's finalised.

Protect yourself against the possibility of your ex maxing out a credit card that's in your name. If you are the primary cardholder, you will be solely responsible for the debts he or she racks up. If you struggle to repay them, it could knock your credit score down. It can be a smart move to ask your credit card issuer for a new card with a different account number. This will leave you without a card for up to 10 days, so make sure you can get by financially until a new card is issued.

All this sounds very dramatic – and maybe you and your ex will part on good terms, but a few precautions can't hurt. Separation can quickly become a battleground, and all bets are off when it comes to assuming your ex will be reasonable.

The main point is that an unhappy relationship can drag down every aspect of your life, and you don't have to stick with it even if you're struggling to scrape some cash together. Make no mistake, divorce often hits women much harder financially than men, especially if children are involved, and it may take time to get back on your feet but there is a whole range of support services to help you along the way.

# Checklist

☐ *Plan the basics for your new life – where you will live, what you'll do for income and how you'll meet costs.*

☐ *Open a bank account in your own name to grow secret savings.*

☐ *Change the PIN and password of any accounts already held in your name.*

☐ *If you have joint accounts, contact the bank and ask that two signatures be required for any transactions.*

☐ *If your partner has a credit card where the account is held in your name, cancel the card.*

☐ *Gather documents like bank statements, passport, tax records and loan statements.*

☐ *Get legal advice – if you can't afford a private lawyer, Legal Aid is available.*

## LET'S GET REAL ...

It's a bit rich to be crying poor if you're decked out in designer clothes, have a kid in private school and get around in a Porsche. I'm not buying it for one minute, but I completely get it if you say you can't save a cent. One thing I learnt a long time ago is that the grass may be greener on the other side but chances are it's fake.

As I was watching a school football game a few years ago, one mother came up to me and said she had just purchased a book about saving and making money. I did question why she would need to read such a book: she is a lawyer and her husband was high up in the finance industry, so I was pretty sure they were flush with cash. Her response was simple: "We can't save a cent!" As she drove out of the car park in the latest Porsche Cayenne, it got me thinking that earning a six-figure salary may still be a sign of status and success but it doesn't mean you're immune from financial woes. Whether you're earning $150,000 or $60,000, there are some very simple reasons why you can't save a cent and money may have nothing to do with it.

# 14

## I earn $150k, why am I still broke?

# Fast fact

ABS statistics show that the average Australian household had a net worth of $1.04 million in 2019-2020 but the wealthiest 20% had an average net worth of $3.27 million.

## IF YOU'RE NOT HAPPY WITH YOUR FINANCIAL SITUATION AND YOU'RE EARNING A DECENT INCOME, IT'S TIME TO ASK YOURSELF SOME TOUGH QUESTIONS – AND I'M NOT TALKING ABOUT WHERE YOU ARE SPENDING BUT WHY YOU ARE SPENDING.

Money is intrinsically linked to our emotions. Most of us probably get this. We know that if we're stressed we look for relief (Bellini, anyone?); if we're not feeling that beautiful we look for things that make us feel good (shoes do it for me); and if we're feeling a little blue we look for things that make us happy.

Given the complexity of why we do what we do, I thought it best to get the help of a behavioural economist – even better, a behavioural economist who's also a psychologist. Phil Slade is just that! He's had more than 15 years' experience in the industry and is also author of Going ApeS#!t and co-founder of Decida.

His insights were invaluable for this chapter and I thank him for that.

## The problem with earning a great income

When you're earning six figures, there's probably not as much pressure to track your spending, which may explain why you're feeling broke. But Phil says the answer may be more about feeling exhausted.

"Whether it is working in a stressful job or simply not getting enough sleep, when we are tired we are more likely to spend money to avoid doing 'painful' or effortful things like cleaning, property maintenance or food prep. We're even more likely to spend more on modes of escapism like entertainment and alcohol. These relatively small expenses can have a huge impact on savings."

This cycle – where we need to work longer hours to increase our income, which then leads us to spend more on products and services, in turn forcing us to earn even more money – is a vicious one that I'm sure plenty of us can relate to.

So why do we trap ourselves in this cycle? Phil says it's because our actions are now locked on autopilot.

"Scientifically, why we become mentally exhausted is explained as bounded rationality or limited cognitive capacity, which basically means that our brain has a finite amount of thinking energy before it needs to recharge, and once you've spent your thinking energy, if you don't allow yourself to recharge, your decision-making gets set to autopilot."

# Why can somebody on $50k save as much as somebody on $100k?

I understand how somebody on $50k may be able to save as much as somebody on $100k. On $50k you're probably young, starting out with no debt, at least not as much as a 40-year-old with two kids. And if you're like most 20-somethings who are serious about saving, you're quite happy to share accommodation, maybe even rent a couch and just live on two-minute noodles.

But assuming we are talking about two people of similar age, stage and circumstance, how is it possible for the lower income earner to be able to save more? When I asked Phil this question, he said that a "fascinating psychological phenomenon comes into play here – it is a problem of relativity, it is a struggle with loss aversion. Basically, if someone on $50,000 (@ $961.54pw) considers spending $500, the pain of the loss relative to their income is much greater than the loss felt by the person on $100,000 (@ $1923.08pw) when considering the same $500 purchase. Therefore, because a large part of our spending consists of many smaller purchases, the person on $100,000 is likely to spend more because it doesn't feel so painful when each 'loss' seems small relative to their overall income (rather than the immediate state of their bank account). This can have the effect of making money more fluid and harder to save. The person on $50,000 feels a greater pain for every small purchase, making money less fluid and therefore easier to track and save."

## Triggers & fixes

The good news is that it is possible to change your money behaviours. The trick is to see saving as a skill rather than an intellectual competency. This way you know that if you practise you will get better.

"If you want to start running, you don't just enter a marathon; you train and see yourself slowly improving. If you started with the marathon you would simply fail and then never try to run again, living with the belief that you can't," says Phil. Finances are the same; you can just say, "I'm no good when it comes to money." Often there is a reason why you do what you do and this can come down to the triggers that trip you up. A trigger is simply something that encourages you to spend money needlessly. Emotions are the general culprits for setting off triggers but things like easy credit and a simple sale can be, too.

While there is nothing wrong with acting on your emotions, they need to be acted on debt free. If it doesn't fit within your budget, best you substitute spending with something to help celebrate or make yourself feel better.

"In the long run, giving into these things that trigger your spending will only make you struggle with your budget or lead you into a great deal of debt down the road. You must learn to control your emotions. If we can't keep our emotions in check, then we're unlikely to be able to keep our spending in check either," says Phil.

*Here are five triggers to watch out for and Phil's solutions to not tripping up.*

**TRIGGER 1: I HAD A SHITTY DAY.** Whether it's because of work deadlines, the stress of getting the kids to school and then coming into work an hour late, a fight with your partner or just not feeling 100%, stress can definitely trigger your spending. You are looking for a distraction to take away the pain.

A similar thing happens if you have a great day. Sometimes you just want to celebrate feeling great. Maybe a pay rise got you in a good mood, you reached your sales target or you've managed to take your lunch into work every day this week. The attitude of "I deserve it!" often justifies a spending binge.

*So what do you do?* Organise dinner with friends on Saturday night even though you can't afford it. Hit the shops for a quick retail fix … whatever takes the stress away or heightens your feelings of joy.

*What Phil suggests you do:* Trick yourself with multiple accounts. He suggests splitting your bank account into multiple accounts and naming them for specific purposes. It limits spending to the account you have your card attached to, it highlights the consequences of robbing one account that's earmarked for a particular expense and it means you are less likely to spend large amounts. This last impact is fascinating, because although it doesn't make rational sense, if we have 10 accounts with $1000 in each, it feels as if we have less than if we had a single account with $10,000 in it. Therefore, spending $500 out of an account with $1000 in it feels like more of a hit than spending $500 out of an account with $10,000 in it. In the first instance, you have lost 50% of your money and in the second you've only parted with 5%. This phenomenon is called mental accounting – we just seem to be wired to need to put things in "buckets". While it may make financial sense to put all your money in one high-interest account, it doesn't always make good human behaviour sense.

**TRIGGER 2: I'M NOWHERE NEAR MY CREDIT LIMIT OR I CAN BUY IT NOW AND PAY FOR IT LATER.** Credit cards and "buy now and pay later" services give us an easy way out. You know you don't have the money to buy it but somehow you justify it. "I've got some money owing to me so I can pay the card off then." "I only need to put down a small deposit and I can pay it off slowly."

It's all about instant gratification and because we're not parting with cash we don't feel the pain! And while "buy now and pay later" services aren't credit cards, these digital disrupters are tempting us to shop more because it's so much easier to buy something you think you have to have when you only need to pay $50 a fortnight rather than $200 upfront. I almost bought something this way when buy now pay later had just come out but I decided to wait and save. Funny thing is, when I had saved the cash I just couldn't justify the spend.

*So what do you do?* Spend without guilt but know that buyer's remorse will kick in when your statements come.

*What Phil suggests you do:* If you do want to buy something you can't afford, resist the urge to go into a repayment scheme. The first thing to do is create what I call a self-made lay-by system. Figure out what the weekly repayments would be and put that amount each week into a separate account until you've saved up the purchase price (or at least a large portion of the purchase price if it's an expensive item like a car). This will save you money on interest, test whether you can afford the repayments, help you avoid credit traps, and give you time to think more rationally about the purchase. Another thing to do is to plan ahead for when you will be tempted by an "impulse" buy that will put you into debt by intentionally putting some "resistance" in the purchase process. For instance, set up a rule with your partner (so you can be held accountable) where any credit or debt purchase needs to be discussed with someone not emotionally involved in the purchase. It needs to be someone who won't directly benefit or get personal gratification from the purchase. This conversation or "credit purchase check" is putting resistance in the purchase process and reduces the emotionally reactive desire for instant gratification.

**TRIGGER 3: I LIVE THROUGH SOCIAL MEDIA.** Social media isn't just eating your data but your wallet, too. One study to come out of the US by two business school researchers found that social media really can influence the amount of money you spend, with Pinterest singled out as the platform likely to make you spend the most.

# If you only do one thing...

Accept yourself: "Learn to be okay with your station in life, to be more than your financial status and you will inevitably stop spending in ways that make you feel guilty. You start controlling your finances rather than them controlling you," says human behaviour expert Phil Slade.

*Did you know?*

*On feeling guilty when you spend: "Guilt and shame are poisonous emotions that never amount to anything good. It's only when you get to a place of grace and contentment that you are ready to make positive changes and start designing your financial future," says Phil Slade.*

*So what do you do?* A glass of red wine, a credit card by your side and you're off! In browsing from one social platform to another, your visionary sensors are in overload and for whatever reason you feel the need to furnish your home with cushions because, hey, your bed can never have too many cushions, right?

*What Phil suggests you do:* Try cutting up your credit cards and disconnecting from social media. "Seriously. Unrealistic social comparisons and easy access to credit are a dangerous mix. Often I hear the following scenario: check Facebook – feel inadequate. Click on an online shopping site – buy something to feel good again. Feel guilty about spending money – retreat to Facebook to feel connected. And so on. Avoid situations that make you feel worthless. Social media can do this. When you feel worthless you are often likely to act in ways to replenish your sense of worth. It's why some people buy a cream bun after going to the gym or buy countless coffees a day to escape a depressing office. Do yourself a favour and construct your environment in a way that helps you. When it's a negative environment you can't escape (such as a stressful home life), increase your awareness of your emotional reactivity in the environment and find ways to restore your self-worth that doesn't require spending money."

**TRIGGER 4: BUT IT'S ON SALE!** Our brain does funny things when we see a 40-70% off sale. We start focusing on the savings rather than the spending. Throw in free shipping, "limited offer" or "only one left" and we jump on it!

*So what do you do?* Buy it, of course! "I'm saving 70%."

*What Phil suggests you do:* There is an old negotiation saying that goes "if you can't walk away from a deal then you won't get a good deal". Picture yourself walking away from the purchase and see if life goes on. If so, then maybe you should let it go. Still want to buy it? Then try mitigating the effects of "anchoring" – a little trick retailers use to present a number directly preceding a sale price (the "original" price or RRP) in order for our brains to judge how valuable something is. The higher the number presented, the higher the perceived value, the more people will pay for something. Avoid being tricked by using your phone to search other stores for the price of the item. Psychologically this "anchors" you to a more realistic number and gives you a better idea of the real value. If you do find it cheaper elsewhere, tell yourself,

"This will be my gift to myself in a few days." Finding relevant information and practising 'delaying gratification' reduces FOMO, stops you making impulse buys, and changes the 'loss' equation to focus on how much you are losing out of your account, as opposed to losing out on a great deal.

**TRIGGER 5: KEEPING UP WITH THE JONESES!** When we earn more we are more likely to gravitate to communities which reflect our income, or our aspirational income at least. Within these communities there are unspoken norms that influence the type of car you drive, the type of clubs you belong to, the events you go to, the way you spend your recreational time, how lavishly you entertain, even the expected price of a good cup of coffee.

*So what do you do?* You keep up with appearances, spending loads of money until you can't afford those "necessary" luxuries.

*What Phil suggests you do:* Have a savings buddy or share your goals. "We need to learn to be content with who we are and our real socio-economic status. The greater the distance between the selves we present to others and our 'real' selves, the greater the chances we will make poor decisions that compound our financial stress. Resist the fear of being judged and revel in the fact that you are getting better, rather than focusing on how much worse off you think you are relative to someone else. Imagine if we created savings groups that acted like running groups, where we shared our savings progress and congratulated each other simply for improving on our monthly personal best? Imagine that!"

A word on emotional spending: Phil talks about having a 500kg ape strapped to our back that we can't see and often forget is there. Our ape represents our instinctive, emotional, reactive responses. You can feel your ape rising up when someone speaks against your loved ones, or you see that piece of chocolate cake in the fridge at the end of a long day at work.

"Apes tend to not make good financial decisions," says Phil. "And yet they make nearly all of our financial decisions because money is so strongly linked with our emotions and our sense of self-worth. The last time you bought a house or a car, how much influence did 'it just felt right/good' have on the purchase? You must learn to control your emotions, disempower them; they are not your friends."

# Checklist

- [ ] *Link your emotions to purchases. For one week keep a journal of what you buy. Write what you were feeling when you bought each item.*

- [ ] *Learn what triggers your spending and where possible find a substitute to address those triggers rather than resort to spending.*

- [ ] *If you can't find a substitute, hold off at least 24 hours before you spend your money.*

- [ ] *Share your money goals with your partner or friend(s) and set up what Phil Slade calls SMART goals (Specific, Measurable, Attainable, Relevant and Timely).*

- [ ] *Accept your financial station in life and never apologise for what you can or can't afford.*

- [ ] *Stay away from negativity.*

## LET'S GET REAL ...

I like to think I'm curious, creative and innovative ... all great attributes of an entrepreneur but I can't claim to be one – an intrapreneur, on the other hand, maybe! Plenty of Aussies can though. The pandemic created something of an entrepreneur boom and it seems like the new Aussie dream is to be your own boss. For some, there was no choice. Their hours were cut or they lost their job, so turning to self-employment was a matter of survival. For others, the pandemic opened up the door for new and expanded business opportunities.

Sure, you miss out on the perks of getting paid to go on leave and your boss topping up your super but what you miss out on there, you gain tenfold elsewhere. I can appreciate the sense of pride and accomplishment gained by turning an idea into a reality. Do it well and you can buy those cushions for yourself.

# CHAPTER

# 15

*I'm sick of working for somebody else*

# Fast fact

337,776 small businesses began operating in 2021-2022 – 241,885 had no employees, 89,286 had one to four employees and 6,605 had five to 19.

## AT SOME STAGE OR ANOTHER I'D SAY MOST PEOPLE HAVE FANTASISED ABOUT QUITTING THEIR JOB AND BECOMING THEIR OWN BOSS.

For some it might be a fleeting thought when they've had a bad week at work and want to tell their boss to shove it but for others it's a real dream to do their own thing. If you're thinking about starting your own business there are two key questions you need to ask yourself: are you doing it for the right reasons and do you have what it takes?

You will probably work much harder and for longer hours when starting your own business than you ever did as an employee, so it's vital that you're doing it for the right reasons. If you're just sick of your job, the people you work with or the hours you're putting in, then maybe going out on your own is not the solution. To give yourself the best chance of success, your business should be something you are interested in and feel passionate about and not just something you're doing because you don't want to be doing what you're doing anymore.

Your personality also matters. Some of the common qualities of successful entrepreneurs include passionate, hard-working, self-motivated, decisive, adaptable and resilient. Are these words that can be used to describe you?

## Don't quit your day job

If I haven't scared you off and you're confident you have what it takes, don't hand in your resignation just yet. Keep a regular salary coming in while you do your research on the viability of your idea.

You should start saving as much money as you can to build a cash cushion to tide you over for the first few months – or possibly even longer – before your business starts to make a profit.

Depending on what your business idea is, you may even try to get it off the ground while you're working. Use that time to build your brand's presence. Needless to say, if your business is in competition with your employer this would be a no-no. Even if it isn't, you should make sure you're not breaching your work contract by starting a side business.

# Do your research

The most important step to take is to research your idea. Sure, you might think it's great but do others agree? Ask a wide range of people whether they would buy what you're selling and at the price you have in mind.

You also need to take a good look at your competitors. Find out what they are doing and what prices they are charging. For your business to succeed you'll need to do it better, differently or cheaper – or even all of the above!

You should also develop a marketing strategy. How will you get customers to come to you? Think about what activities will work for your business. Will it be delivering pamphlets, generating interest on social media or something else?

# Have a plan

All your research will help you with your business plan, which is a vital tool. It is like a road map that can show you where you are going and how to get there.

You can find business plan templates online that will show you what should be included – things like information about your product, the market and your marketing strategy. Then there will be the financial details such as set-up costs, ongoing costs and cash-flow projections. It should give you a clear picture of how much money you need to get your business off the ground.

The level of detail needed in your plan depends on whether you need to borrow money to get your business up and running. If you need to raise finance it will have to be fairly in-depth to convince a lender to lend you money. If you don't need to borrow money, it is still a worthwhile exercise.

# Show me the money

Your business plan should have helped you come up with the magic figure – the amount you'll need to get it up and running. Don't forget to factor in enough to cover at least six to 12 months of expenses because it might take that long before you start making enough money.

If you have the amount saved up, that's great. If not then you need to think about where the money will come from. Credit cards are not a great idea as you'll need to pay back the debt too quickly. If you have equity in your home you could try borrowing against that.

# Need To know

One of the hardest things about running your own business is achieving a good work-life balance. Planning what hours you'll work and sticking to it is one way to prevent your business taking over your life. And don't try to do everything yourself. Once your business is making some money, employ a staff member to help out or outsource tasks such as bookkeeping.

If not then you'll need to apply for a business loan. This won't be easy and you'll probably have to jump through quite a few hoops.

In general, lenders look at three areas: your credentials (if you have no experience in the business it makes lenders nervous), the business's ability to service the debt and the security on offer. Often it's a lack of security that lets down budding businesses.

If you don't meet these traditional lending guidelines, there are alternatives. You might consider a peer-to-peer loan but it may come with a premium interest rate. If all else fails there are friends, family and even private investors to fall back on. Many successful businesses have started off this way but they don't come without their own pitfalls.

## Your start-up checklist

So the time has come to turn your business from an idea into a reality. There are a few things you'll need to cross off your list to make this happen.

## 1. DECIDE ON A BUSINESS STRUCTURE

You need to decide what business structure you want to use – sole trader, partnership or company – and then make sure this is established properly. If you're unsure try using this tool: register.business.gov.au/helpmedecide.

## 2. APPLY FOR AN ABN AND REGISTER YOUR BUSINESS NAME

Check to make sure the name you have in mind isn't already taken. You can do this at connectonline.asic.gov.au or at business.gov.au. You should also check it's not already a registered trademark, which you can do at ipaustralia.gov.au.

It's also probably worth finding out whether the domain name is available. You don't want to choose a name only to find out later that it is not available. Also check it's available on social media channels.

After you've done all the relevant checks you can apply for an ABN and register the business name at the same time at register.business.gov.au. You will need the ABN to register the name.

## 3. REGISTER YOUR DOMAIN NAME

As soon as you have registered your business name, snap up the domain name even if you don't plan on setting up a website right away. You don't want it to be already taken when you're ready to go online.

# If you only do one thing...

Research as much as possible before you take the leap. Is your product or service one that will sell, and who will buy it? Identify your competitors and how you can stand out from them. Think about the strengths and weaknesses of your idea.

## 4. CHECK IF YOU NEED ANY BUSINESS LICENCES

It's a good idea to find out about any licences and permits you may need to run your business. For example, if you're running a business from home you may need a zoning permit, or if you're opening a restaurant you will need to be registered as a food premises. The list is long and depends on the type of business you're running. You can find more details at ablis.business.gov.au.

## 5. DO YOU NEED TO REGISTER FOR GST?

If you expect your annual turnover to be $75,000 or more, you have to register for GST. If the turnover will be less than $75,000, it's optional. It is hard to know for sure what your turnover will be. You can keep track and if it looks as if you're likely to exceed the threshold, you can register then.

You can register online at ato.gov.au, phone the tax office on 132 866 or go through your registered tax agent.

If you do register for GST you will have to charge customers GST and you'll be able to claim GST on your business purchases. You must stay registered for at least 12 months. It will mean more admin work because you'll have to file quarterly business activity statements (BAS) with the tax office.

## 6. OPEN A SEPARATE BANK ACCOUNT

Opening a separate bank account for your business is also a good idea. It will make it easier to keep records and do your tax returns. It will also let you keep better track of how your business is going. To manage cash flow you may opt to take out a business credit card as well.

## 7. GET THE RIGHT INSURANCE

Insurance for your business is a must. Consider public liability insurance because it will cover personal injury or property damage sustained by visitors or clients on your premises. If you offer advice you may also think about professional indemnity insurance. You should also protect your assets, including your property, contents and stock, from fire, theft, breakdowns, etc. Business interruption insurance is another good idea. If a fire damages your property and you can't trade, you'll be covered. It may help to use a broker to work out what type of cover you need. If you're running a business from home, make sure you tell your insurer because you may have to take out separate cover. Don't just assume your existing policy will protect you.

# Checklist

☐ *Make sure you're starting your business for the right reasons and you have what it takes to succeed.*

☐ *Keep working in your current job while you research, save money and build your brand.*

☐ *Do your research on the product and service and your competition, and develop a marketing strategy.*

☐ *Have a solid business plan to help you on the path to success.*

☐ *Work out where you'll get the money to make it happen.*

☐ *Get all your paperwork sorted – register your business name and domain, get an ABN, register for GST, etc.*

☐ *Protect your brand – for example, do you need a patent or trademark?*

☐ *Open a separate bank account.*

☐ *Take out the necessary insurance to protect your business.*

☐ *Get help if you need it.*

## LET'S GET REAL ...

When I hit the big 67 I don't want my budget to dictate to me that it's polyester and cask wine from here on. In fact, it's one of my biggest fears. I don't want to slow down in retirement and I'm not talking about my pace. If you're enjoying the finer things in life right now, why should retirement put an end to that? Of course you need to ask yourself how you will fund it?

As you'll find out in this chapter, working out the cost of your lifestyle in retirement isn't that hard. The issue we face as women is that we live longer. I never thought I'd complain about that but here's why. A quick play around on a longevity calculator had me living anywhere from 81 (that's when I was honest about my drinking habits) to 91 (different calculator) to 96 (another calculator) then 102 (went back and changed some answers, that is I haven't had a speeding fine in the past 12 months and I don't stress). I must say I was a little frightened about living to 102 because, frankly, I know I won't have enough money to make it until then. The good news is that there are plenty of options to help you fund your lifestyle.

# CHAPTER

# 16

How much will I really need in retirement?

# Fast fact

*In 2018-2019, 36% of retired women relied on their partner's income to meet their living costs at retirement (compared to 7% of retired men), according to the ABS.*

## WE HEAR SO MUCH ABOUT WHAT WE SHOULD BE DOING TO PLAN FOR RETIREMENT – BUILD INVESTMENTS, GROW SUPER, PAY OFF THE MORTGAGE.

Yet very few people have any idea about how much they really need in retirement. That's amazing when you think about it because we could spend 20, maybe 30 years in retirement.

Part of the problem is that every expert you come across seems to have a different idea of how much you'll need in retirement. I've come across claims that you should have sufficient savings to provide an income equal to 70%-80% of your final salary. I've seen a rule of thumb that says you should have $15 saved for each $1 of annual income you want in retirement. In other words, you'll need $750,000 stashed away to have a yearly income of $50,000. I've even read some hair-raising suggestions that we need a minimum of $1 million to afford a decent retirement. That's certainly not going to happen for most of us!

One guide that's often quoted is the retirement standard regularly published by the Association of Superannuation Funds of Australia (ASFA). It estimates that a couple hoping for a "comfortable" retirement will need $640,000 in savings, or $545,000 if you're single. If you're pitching for a more modest retirement, ASFA says both couples and singles will need just $70,000. This assumes the age pension will cover a large chunk of regular living costs.

Consumer advocacy organisation, Super Consumers Australia (SCA), also has its own estimates. It found a single person with a medium level of spending will need $301,000 and a couple will need $402,000. Both ASFA's and SCA's estimates assume you own your house outright at retirement. If you're renting or still have a mortgage it's a different story.

Of course, these averages are all very interesting but they are not you. They just form guidelines in the same way that the typical family supposedly consists of 2.2 children and 15% of a labrador. While I can't tell you exactly how much money you will need, by putting three simple factors together – the annual cost of your lifestyle in retirement, the planned date of your retirement and your life expectancy – you'll have a much clearer picture of how much money you may need. Don't panic if the number seems overwhelming because we'll see later that there are a number of sources where the cash can come from.

$1 + 2 + 3 =$ retirement

## 1. WHAT WILL YOUR RETIREMENT LOOK LIKE?

If you see yourself living a retirement filled with round-the-world travel, fine dining and memberships to expensive golf clubs, it's a no-brainer that you're going to need a lot more in savings than someone who plans to fill their days pottering in the garden and enjoying Friday nights with a sit-down at the local bowlo.

That's why the starting point to working out how much you need to fund involves working backwards to look forwards. By that I mean thinking about what you want from retirement – and, more to the point, how much that lifestyle is going to cost. The more you can break down the details of your retirement lifestyle, the better. If you're serious about knowing how much you'll need, start to jot down plans for what you want life after work to look like.

Start with essential spending on things like food, clothing, transport and utilities. Then decide the nice-to-haves like dining out, holidays and hobbies. The final factor to look at is the luxuries. Would you like a boat or caravan? Are you planning to help with your grandkids' school fees?

Remember that some things may work in your favour in retirement. The amount of tax you have to pay may be reduced thanks to the seniors and pensioners tax offset. The kids will have left home, or at least be nearing the tail end of their education, so the bulk of costs associated with raising kids will be behind you and if you own your home it will either be paid off or close to it.

It's not hard to cost the lifestyle you want, and with not much effort you should end up with an idea of how much you need to live on each year in retirement.

## 2. WHEN WILL YOU RETIRE?

Technically there is no specific age in Australia when you must retire. If you're willing and able to do so, there may be nothing to stop you from working well into your nineties. One benchmark to use for retirement is the date when you can access your super. That's 60 if you were born after July 1, 1964.

Or you may want to hold off until you can access the age pension. From July 1, 2023 that is 67.

Working for longer isn't everyone's cup of tea but it can help you retire stronger. Not only does it give you more time to grow your super, it also cuts short the time that you're drawing on your savings. The thing is, there are no guarantees about when we retire. Poor health and redundancy can quickly put paid to plans to work for as long as possible, so it pays to be flexible.

## 3. YOUR LIFE EXPECTANCY

One area where women have it all over men is life expectancy. Broadly speaking, women today can expect to live to 85 (men can expect to live for about four years less). That's not to say every woman will pass away at 85. Some will live far longer, some less.

There's no sure way of knowing how long you will live. Your family's health history can be a big influencer. So is your lifestyle. One way to predict your life expectancy is with an online calculator. The Death Clock (death-clock.org) is actually quite fun to use. It asks only seven questions, so it takes a couple of seconds to get a result, but it gives you the exact date you'll pass away. Something cheery to mark on the calendar.

Why does life expectancy matter? Well, it's a big deal when it comes to retirement planning. If you come from a family where everyone is blessed with good genes, you could live to a ripe old age and possibly spend decades in retirement. That's fantastic if you've got some money behind you to whoop it up. But it's a heck of a long time if you're constantly strapped for cash and trying to live off the age pension. If you're not convinced, bear in mind that the maximum basic age pension for a single person is worth just over $450 a week. Try living off that for a while and chances are you'll soon see that it will keep you stocked in tea and crackers but not much more.

The upshot is that the longer your life expectancy, the more you may need in savings to tide you over to a very old age.

# Bring it all together

The final step to knowing how much you need for retirement is to bring together the three factors we've just looked at — the annual cost of your dream lifestyle, retirement date and life expectancy.

Let's say, for instance, that you do the sums and find your retirement lifestyle will cost $35,000 annually. If you plan to retire at 67 and have a life expectancy of about 85, you could be looking at 18 years in retirement. On that basis you'll need around $630,000 to fund your lifestyle. Or you could find it's going to cost you $80,000 each year, in which case you'll need about $1.44 million.

Don't reach for the smelling salts just yet! You see, there's a key factor we've left out of the picture — and that's investment returns. As long as you don't stash your savings under the bed, your money is going to earn a return.

Let's say your portfolio earns 4% to 5%pa on average (some years it will be more, some years it will be less). If you've got $630,000 in savings, it could earn $25,000 to $31,000 each year — there's your annual income. If you've got $1.44 million, you could earn $57,000 to $72,000 each year. If you need more, take a bit out of your capital. Yes, it will see the value of your nest egg fall as you age. And if you're worried about what you'll leave the kids, let them have the house.

At this point you're probably thinking: "Uh oh … Effie's hit the cask wine early, because I don't have $600,000, let alone $1.4 million." Fair point. The good news here is that even if you have a modest nest egg, there's a whole variety of potential income sources in retirement, and they're just waiting to be tapped.

# Coming up with money to live on in retirement

During our working days we rely heavily on one main source of income — usually our wage or salary. In retirement you're more likely to have a patchwork of different inflows that all go towards funding your lifestyle. It's important to know what the different options are because together they can get you over the line and into your preferred lifestyle. It's a good idea to get independent expert advice around this.

# Need to know

*Make sure you plan for aged care. Hopefully you will be able to stay at home for a long time but there may come a time when you'll need extra support. That might be help at home or moving to an aged care facility, which can be surprisingly expensive.*

## YOUR SUPER

Super is specifically designed to provide money to live on in retirement, so for most of us it will be the key source of income. And, yes, it is definitely worth adding to it while you're in the workforce. The more money you can whack in now, the more you will have to spend in retirement.

The first step is to know how much money you're likely to have in super by the time you quit the workforce. Most super funds feature an online calculator on their web page or take a look at the online retirement planner on the MoneySmart website.

If it turns out you'll have far less than expected, you can ramp up the balance with extra contributions. There are also tips on how to boost your super without even adding in a cent in Chapter 8 ("Who's got spare cash to contribute to super?").

## The retirement sweet spot

Surprisingly, having too much in super could end up working against you. Analysis by ETF provider BetaShares found that for Australians at retirement age with savings of between $350,000 and $600,000, increasing their savings may result in their income decreasing.

This is because of something referred to as the "retirement trap" or "taper rate trap". The taper rate is essentially the rate by which your age pension entitlement reduces based on the value of your assets. For every $1000 of assets above the lower threshold, retirees lose $3 from their fortnightly pension

According to the Alliance for a Fairer Retirement System, the current taper rate creates a "sweet spot" for retirees to reduce their savings in order to receive the full age pension. It estimates that sweet spot to be around $400,000 in savings. This sees a pensioner couple earning $1000 a month more than a couple with $800,000 in savings.

## Lump sum or pension?

You can access your super when you turn 65 (even if you haven't retired) or when you reach preservation age and retire. Your preservation age ranges from 55 to 60, depending on when you were born. For anyone born after July 1, 1964 it is 60. (You may also be able to access it when you hit your preservation age and still continue to work under the transition to retirement rules. More on this option later.)

There are two main ways to access the money – either by withdrawing a lump sum, or by using a private pension to receive regular payments.

Taking your super as a lump sum may sound tempting but it means shifting the money out of a tax-friendly environment and into one where any returns can be fully taxed. Not a good move. Unless you really need the money as a lump sum – for example, to pay off a big debt like your home loan, you're better off leaving it in the super system and gradually drawing it down as an income stream.

## THE AGE PENSION

Around 62% of Australia's over-65s rely on a full or part age pension to fund their retirement. That proportion is so large partly because the income and asset limits for the pension are pretty generous.

As a guide, in 2022 you can still receive a part payment of the age pension if you own assets worth up to $609,250 for a single or $915,500 combined for a couple. This assumes you own your home; the limits are higher if you're not a homeowner. An income test also applies but you can earn up to $2165.20 each fortnight as a single or $3313.60 combined for a couple and be eligible for a part payment. The cut-off limits are higher for those who get the work bonus.

As I write in late 2022, the maximum base rate for the age pension is $900.80 per fortnight for a single person and $1358 for a couple. Disregarding annual increases, over 20 years that fortnightly payment could add up to around $468,000 for a single and roughly $706,000 for a couple. It's easy to see how the age pension can make a significant difference in helping you lead an enjoyable retirement even if your savings are on the lean side.

I'm certainly not suggesting that the age pension is going to fund a ritzy retirement but it's good to know it offers a fall-back position or at least an income top-up. And even if you only earn a part pension, you're entitled to discounts on a variety of household bills, from medicines to car rego.

# If you only do one thing...

*Cost your retirement. It basically boils down to the number of years you'll be in retirement multiplied by your annual cost of living. And if the figure you arrive at seems unachievable, remember there are a variety of different sources you can draw on to make up your overall annual income.*

But here's the thing. This is how the pension stands today. Given our ageing society, there's no telling what will happen with the age pension in the future but it's a fair bet that it will become harder to qualify for it. That's why I'm a big fan of taking steps to grow your super. Yes, the rules governing super change regularly, and understandably that rattles people. But it's still the best option for controlling how much you have to live on in retirement.

## OTHER INVESTMENTS

Super is more of a certainty, thanks to compulsory employer contributions, than independently grown investments but if you have built up assets outside of super these can also be used to provide money in retirement. This might be a share portfolio, ETFs, fixed interest or even property.

One advantage of investing outside of super for your retirement is that you don't have to meet the same "conditions of release" you do with super. So if you want to stop working early you will be able to use your investments to help cover your costs.

*What if you don't have enough?*

The median super balance for women aged between 60-64 is about $139,000 – it's not a huge amount to last what could be a 20-year retirement. Happily, there are other sources of cash beyond super that you can tap into in retirement. If you are getting closer to retirement but you don't think your super will give you the retirement lifestyle you want – even after you add in any age pension you're entitled to – here are a few options.

## WORK PART TIME, TOP UP WITH SUPER

Another way to boost your super is to put off retiring for a bit longer. Quite simply, the fewer the number of years between when you stop working and when you die, the less money you need.

That doesn't have to mean slogging away full time into your 70s. It's possible to access your super even if you haven't completely hung up your work heels. If you're working part time, a transition to retirement pension (TTR) can be used to top up your income using funds from your super. You will need to have reached your preservation age (that's 60 if you were born after July 1, 1964) and, to ensure you don't blow your super before you have retired, the money can only be taken as a series of regular payments, not a lump sum.

A TTR can help you maintain your lifestyle even if you switch to part-time or casual work to ease your way into retirement. But it can mean eating into your super before you quit work altogether, especially if you are drawing down more than your employer is putting in. So think carefully about dipping into your super early.

Keeping a hand in the workforce even during retirement can pay dividends. If you're eligible for the age pension, under the work bonus scheme you can earn up to $300 a fortnight without affecting your pension. Basically, you have a $300 work bonus available each fortnight. If you don't use it, it is accumulated in an "income bank" up to a maximum amount of $7800 a year. The amount in the income bank offsets future income from work that would normally be assessable under the pension income test. There's no time limit – the income bank amount keeps carrying forward if it isn't used.

It's not a bad deal, especially as work also provides other valuable benefits such as mental stimulation and social contact.

## YOUR HOME

Your home can be an unexpected source of cash in your senior years. In fact, it's in retirement that the effort of paying down a mortgage can really reap dividends. Not only does it mean that you don't have to worry about finding money for loan repayments, which can be a real cash drain, it also gives you options about ways to use your home to generate extra income – and I'm not talking about advertising the spare bedroom on Airbnb (though that is always an option).

### Downsize your home – upsize your super

Downsizing can free up a truckload of home equity and potentially let you enjoy a lower-maintenance lifestyle, which is something that can be really important as we age. Or maybe you can move to a location closer to the things you want to be near – be it your favourite spot up the coast or somewhere close to inner-city cafes and shops. However, downsizing also means paying stamp duty and legal fees on a new place, and these costs can eat heavily into your retirement money.

Again there is no right or wrong answer, especially as selling the family home comes with far more of an emotional wrench than offloading a few shares. That said, there is a financial incentive to consider downsizing. Homeowners aged 60 and older can make a downsizer super contribution of up to $300,000.

That limit applies to each owner, so if you own your place as part of a couple, you could potentially boost your combined super savings by up to $600,000. Downsizer contributions are tax free, and they won't count towards contributions caps. Even if your super balance is greater than the transfer balance cap (currently $1.7 million), you can still take advantage of the downsizer contribution. However, they will count towards the transfer balance cap.

The big stumbling block is that downsizing could change your eligibility for the age pension. Once you have sold your home and purchased a new place, you could be left with substantial funds to invest. That's great news but it could put you over the age pension assets limit.

That may not be an issue if you previously only just scraped in for a part pension. It's a different matter, though, if it sees you suddenly catapulted into being a self-funded retiree.

The main point is that it's an option to free up money for retirement but it's worth getting advice to know if it's the right choice for you.

## Take out a reverse mortgage

If you don't fancy the idea of selling up and moving, a reverse mortgage can let you dip into the value of your home while you're still living there. They work like this: equity in the home is converted into cash either through the payment of a lump sum, a regular income stream or a combination of both.

How much you can borrow comes down to the value of your home and your age. Generally, the older you are the more you can borrow. Typically, a 60-year-old is able to borrow around 15%-20%. As a guide, add 1% for each year over 60, suggests MoneySmart. Minimum and maximum amounts will differ among lenders.

The real clincher is that no repayments are necessary until you pass away or sell up to move into aged care. This means that unlike "forward mortgages", where principal and interest repayments reduce the debt, reverse mortgages keep climbing. Interest and fees are added to the debt.

The compounding effect of interest charges means the debt will usually double every 10 years. This impact could be reduced if your lender allows you to draw down amounts as needed rather than taking a lump sum upfront.

It's worth noting that reverse mortgages taken out after September 2012 have "negative equity protection", which means you can't end up owing the lender more than your home is worth.

That doesn't mean you won't lose any equity. Just how much you'll lose and how fast depends on three factors: the future value of your home, how much you borrow and when, and the rate and fees on the loan. The MoneySmart website has a reverse mortgage calculator you can play around with.

It is important to get advice on how a reverse mortgage could impact your age pension and your estate. The main downside may be that your kids might not get as big an inheritance as they were expecting but what child is going to begrudge you a decent retirement lifestyle?

## Use the Home Equity Access Scheme

An alternative to a reverse mortgage is the government's Home Equity Access Scheme (formerly the Pension Loans Scheme) run through Services Australia. It works in a similar way to a reverse mortgage. You need to use equity in real estate you own in Australia as security for the loan – it doesn't necessarily have to be the home you live in.

To be eligible you or your partner have to be age pension age or older. You also must be getting a qualifying pension (the age pension, carer payment or disability support pension) or at least be eligible for one of them. You might meet the rules, for example, but your rate is zero because your income or assets are over the threshold, explains Services Australia.

The maximum you can borrow depends on your age (or if you have a younger partner it is based on their age) and your security for the loan. If you get a pension, your combined loan and pension payment each fortnight can't be more

# Need to know

One of the perks of getting older is that you may be entitled to a range of discounts, rebates and concessions. These include cheaper insurance, energy rebates and concessional travel. The National Seniors website has a calculator that can help you work out what concessions you may be eligible for.

than 150% of your maximum pension rate. If you don't get a pension, you can borrow up to 150% of the maximum age pension.

You can choose to get the money as a fortnightly payment, as a lump sum or a combination of both.

At the time of writing, the rate was 3.95% and it compounds each fortnight on the loan balance until you repay the loan in full. So the longer you take to repay the loan, the more interest you'll pay.

If you end up selling the house you have used as security, you can transfer the loan to another property or repay the loan on the date of settlement. If you die, Services Australia will usually recover any outstanding loan from your estate. Interest will continue to accrue until the loan is repaid.

## Home reversion or equity release schemes

You may also be able to tap into the equity in your home with a home reversion or equity release scheme. Instead of getting a loan, you actually sell a share of the future sale proceeds of your home in exchange for a lump sum now. You sell your portion for a discounted rate. This option means you don't have to worry about interest capitalising but it still ends up costing you. Let's say your home is worth $500,000 and you sell a 20% share for $75,000. If you sell your home for $750,000, the provider gets $150,000.

It's important to get expert advice if you are considering any of the options discussed in this chapter.

# Checklist

- ☐ *Work out the annual cost of your retirement lifestyle.*

- ☐ *Set the age at which you'd like to retire.*

- ☐ *Get a rough idea of how long you'll live — plenty of online calculators can help here.*

- ☐ *Multiply the number of years you'll be in retirement by the annual cost — that's how much of a nest egg you need.*

- ☐ *Invest your savings — the returns provide money to live on.*

- ☐ *Work for longer where possible.*

- ☐ *Gradually draw down your super.*

- ☐ *Check age pension eligibility.*

- ☐ *Consider using your home to generate income — either through downsizing, a reverse mortgage or the Pension Loans Scheme.*

- ☐ *Get independent expert advice.*

# LET'S GET REAL ...

It's easy to feel overwhelmed about how to take better control of your finances –
especially when high inflation and rising interest rates have made life feel more
expensive than ever.

Sometimes, all you need is someone to break it down for you and show you what
you need to do. That's the idea behind my Bill Buster Action Plan and Money
Makeover. The two go hand in hand and provide a step-by-step guide to giving
your finances an overhaul.

The Bill Buster Action Plan includes a range of tips and tricks to cut the costs
of the everyday bills that seem to be taking a larger chunk out of our budgets.

Then there's the Money Makeover starting on page 213. I've come up with 26
challenges you need to complete. Most of these will help you save or make money.
The others will help you get your financial affairs in order.

Think of it like a game of bingo. Start by picking a task that you want to
complete – there is no specific order, just choose one that you feel like doing. When
it's completed, make a record, including any savings, in the "What I've achieved"
column, cross off the task and then move on to the next one.

You can do this at your own pace. Some weeks you might choose to do nothing
while other weeks you might cross three off the list. It doesn't matter how long
it takes, it just matters that you do it. When you have crossed everything off and
yelled "Bingo!" you'll be happy you did. Your finances will be all the better for it.
Make sure you tally up everything you have saved to see just how much your efforts
have paid off.

# BILL BUSTER ACTION PLAN

*with*

*Money Makeover*

# LIFE CAN BE REALLY EXPENSIVE. IT OFTEN FEELS LIKE THERE'S ONE BILL AFTER ANOTHER TO PAY.

There's the mortgage or rent, electricity and gas, insurance, telco bills, groceries...the list goes on and on. Add to this the fact that inflation has been rising but wage growth has not kept up and it means our budgets are stretched more than ever.

Most of these everyday bills aren't things we can simply "give up" to save money but that doesn't mean we should be paying any more than we have to. That's why I have put together this action plan to help you find ways to cut those costs. Now, I'm not reinventing the wheel here, and there will be tips that you have heard before but having all this information in the one place will hopefully make it easier for you to take action and bust those bills.

## 1. IDENTIFY ALL YOUR REGULAR BILLS

The first step of the process is to make a list of all your regular bills. You can do this by going through your bank or credit card statements. Another option is to use an expense tracker app like Frollo. You can sync the app up to your bank accounts and it will automatically put your expenses into various categories for you, which is easier than going through all your statements.

When you identify all the expenses, be sure to make a note of important info as this will help you with the later steps. Here's a list of the details to jot down:

• *Your mortgage repayments:* the interest rate, any ongoing fees, the fortnightly/monthly repayment and the outstanding balance.

• *Credit card:* the interest rate, annual fee and the outstanding balance.

• *Electricity bills:* the supply charge and the usage rate(s).

• *Car insurance:* the monthly/annual premium, the excess, whether you're insured for market or agreed value.

• *Home and contents insurance:* the monthly/annual premium, the excess and the sum insured.

• *Health insurance:* the monthly/annual premium, the excess and the level of cover, for example, bronze, silver or gold.

• *Internet:* the monthly cost, the NBN speed and the data included.

• *Mobile plan:* the monthly cost and how many GB of data you get each month.

## 2. ANALYSE YOUR FINDINGS

Next, take the time to take a closer look at all the products and services to work out whether they are still right for you. You don't want to be paying for things you don't need. For example, maybe you originally took out gold health insurance because it covered you for obstetrics but your baby-making days are now behind you so you may be able to switch to silver cover. Or maybe your mobile plan includes 20GB of data but you never use more than 5GB.

If you think you may be able to make changes, then add this info to the notes you made in step one.

## 3. LOOK FOR BETTER DEALS

Finding a better deal can be the easiest way to save money and the potential savings can add up to thousands over a year. So, now that you have put together your list of expenses and know exactly how much you're paying it's time to start shopping around to compare prices.

You can use comparison sites such as Canstar (of which I am Editor-at-Large), government sites such as energymadeeasy.gov.au and privatehealth.gov.au, or go directly to various providers' websites.

When you're shopping around, it's vital to compare apples with apples to get a true picture of how the products stack up against each other. That's why I asked you to make the notes in step one.

So, let's say you're looking for a new internet plan, by knowing how much data you have and the NBN speed, you will be able to make sure you are looking at similar products. Of course, if in step two you worked out that you wanted to change things up, then use that info when shopping around.

Remember, you shouldn't sacrifice quality for a cheaper product. For example, you might be able to save on insurance by switching but what use is that to you if you can't use it when it's time to make a claim?

Write down what you find as you'll need this for the next step. For example, what premium were you quoted for your car and home insurance or what was the monthly cost for the cheaper NBN plan?

## 4. APPROACH YOUR EXISTING PROVIDER

If you have found that it's possible to score a better deal, it's a good idea to give your current provider the opportunity to match or beat that price – especially if it will cost you money to switch.

### Gather the information

To give yourself the best chance of success it pays to go in prepared. Have the following information on hand:

• Details about the better deals you have found including price/rate and the name of the provider.

• What your existing provider is offering new customers – maybe it's a cheaper rate or maybe they're throwing in "extras".

• How long you have been with your current provider – if you have been a long-term customer you can use that in your conversation – any issues you have had in the past and whether you have any other services with them.

• Know what you would be willing to accept. If they come close but don't match the better offer, for example, will you stay or walk?

### Make the call

Now, it's time to make the call. There are two ways you can go about this.

The first is to talk to whoever answers the phone and tell them you have found a better deal. If they say they are unable to give you a better price, then tell them you'd like to cancel. They will then likely transfer you to the customer retention department whose role is to hold on to customers so you'll probably have better luck with them.

The second is to cut straight to the chase and ask to speak to someone in the customer retention team.

### Talking points

It can be tricky to know what to say. Here are some phrases to provide you with some inspiration.

• *I've been shopping around and have found better deals from other providers.*
*I'd like to talk to someone about what you may be able to offer me.*

- *I've been checking how my mortgage rate/insurance premium/internet bill compares with what you're offering new customers, and I'm disappointed that my rate/premium/bill is so much higher. What can you do for me?*

- *I saw that you are offering new customers X. How can I take advantage of this offer?*

- *I've been a loyal customer for X years. What's the best you can do?*

- *I have two mobile services/insurance policies with you – can you give me a better rate?*

- *If I brought other products to you, would you be able to give me a bigger discount?*

Make sure you're calm and polite. If you're angry or aggressive it will work against you. At the same time, though, be firm and let them know that you mean business. If they won't come to the party then tell them you'd be willing to walk away. Use phrases like:

- *I'd like the rate you're offering new customers, otherwise, I'm happy to take my business elsewhere.*

- *I have been a loyal customer for X years and although I'd prefer to keep my business with you I can't pass up the deal X is offering.*

- *Unfortunately, if you can't match the deal X is offering I will have to cancel my cover.*

You don't have to follow through if you don't want to. You can say: *Thank you, let me think about it and I'll call back if I decide to take my business elsewhere.*

## 5. MAKE THE SWITCH

If your existing provider doesn't agree to give you a better deal then you should seriously think about taking your business elsewhere. Just be sure to factor in any costs to make sure making the switch is worth it. For example, will you be charged a cancellation fee or is there a setup fee?

In Chapter 5 ("I don't want to live with a mortgage") I wrote about doing a break-even analysis if you are considering refinancing your home loan and the same applies to all other products. You add up any costs associated with switching and divide by the monthly savings. So, let's say you have found an NBN plan that is $10 a month cheaper but you'll have to pay a $50 cancellation fee, it will take you five months to break even.

# Other ways to slash your bills

Finding a better deal might be an easy way to save money but it's not necessarily the only way. Here are some tips.

## Groceries

• Keep an eye out for discounts on gift cards that you can use at the supermarket. Coles and Woolies sometimes have them on special. It's also worth checking with your insurer, motoring organisation, energy or telco company to see if they offer the option to purchase supermarket gift cards for a discount. Discounts can range from 1% to 10%. Assuming you scored a 10% discount, a $100 gift card would cost you just $90 meaning that effectively you'd be able to buy $100 worth of groceries for just $90. Do that every week and the savings can really add up. Just be sure to check any processing fees and find out if there are limits to how many gift cards you can purchase each year.

• Download the HalfPrice app which shows you everything that's 50% off at Coles and Woolworths. When you spot pricier items such as dishwashing tablets, laundry powder or toiletries at half price then take the opportunity to stock up. You can also use grocery price comparison apps such as Frugl to check prices before you head to the supermarket.

• Don't fall into the trap of thinking that because something is on special that it is the best value or that bigger is cheaper. Make sure you look at the unit price when you are comparing prices. This lets you easily compare the prices of products, regardless of their size, brand or the way they are packaged or sold because it uses a standard unit of measurement. So it tells you the cost per litre, per kilogram, per 100gm – whatever applies to the product you're buying. You can find a product's unit price on the shelf label if you're shopping at the supermarket. If you are doing a grocery shop online, you can change your filters so that products are sorted by unit price.

• If you shop at Coles or Woolworths, consider signing up for their rewards program. You earn points each time you shop and when you have built up a certain number of points you can use them to get a discount off your shopping.

• Shop later in the day because you are more likely to be able to score discounts. Often bakery items are marked down at the end of the day and you might find the same happens with meat, fruit and veg.

# Petrol and car costs

- Stack your fuel discounts. Both Coles and Woolworths offer a 4 cents a litre discount on fuel if you spend $30 or more on groceries. You may also be able to get discounts from motoring organisations such as NRMA and RACQ and if you have a Linkt toll account you can also get a discount. You can often combine these discounts to get an even bigger discount. Here's an example: You can use your 4 cents a litre Coles discount at Shell Coles Express stations. Coles Express offers a 10 cents a litre discount if you spend $20 on eligible products in-store. Obviously, you shouldn't buy things just for the discount but think about what you may actually need. Use those together and you'll save 14 cents a litre. If you have a Linkt toll account, you can get a further 4 cents a litre discount, bringing the total savings to 18 cents a litre. Just be sure to check the terms and conditions.

- Lock in your fuel price. The 7-Eleven fuel app lets you search nearby 7-Eleven Stores to find the best current local price for your preferred fuel type. If you find a great price, you can use the app to lock in that price for up to seven days.

- Use a fuel app such as MotorMouth or Fuel Map Australia to find the best price for petrol near you. The difference can be as much as 20 cents a litre between petrol stations only a few kilometres apart.

- If you have waited until the petrol light has come on to fill up you are at the mercy of the petrol cycle. You might find that the price of fuel that day is particularly expensive. If that's the case, then don't fill up the tank. Put in enough to cover you for a few days and wait for prices to come down. The ACCC monitors petrol price cycles so it's worth checking out the site for insights.

- Consider using Premium Unleaded 95 or Standard Unleaded 91 instead of paying more for Premium Unleaded 98. Make sure you check what your car manufacturer recommends you use. This is usually on the fuel flap of your car. If it says "Premium unleaded only" then you shouldn't use 91.

- If you're on a pension, you may be eligible for rebates or concessions on public transport or vehicle registration. In NSW, for example, eligible pensioners don't have to pay registration fees or motor vehicle tax. Check what is on offer in your state or territory.

# Energy bills

• Find out if you are on a single rate tariff or time of use tariff. A time of use tariff means that the price of electricity changes at different times of the day and it will cost more at "peak" times and less at "off-peak" times. If you're on a time of use tariff, then make sure you know what those times are and adjust your behavior accordingly. For example, if peak usage rates are from 2pm to 8pm on weeknights then don't turn the dishwasher on until after 8.

• Make some changes around the home. Use cold water instead of hot when doing the laundry, hang up clothes as much as possible instead of using the dryer, switch appliances off at the wall, make sure to turn the lights off when you leave a room and have shorter showers.

• You may be able to get a discount on your bill if you set up a direct debit, get your bills emailed to you instead of receiving a paper bill or paying on time. Check what's on offer and set things up accordingly.

• Find out if you can save by bundling your services. For example, having both gas and electricity with one provider. Some providers even give you the option to bundle energy and internet.

• If you can't live without the air-con in summer, try to avoid setting the thermostat too low. It is estimated that each degree warmer on the thermostat can save you 10%. The optimum temperature will depend on where you live but in summer aim for no lower than about 25 degrees unless you're in a tropical climate.

# Internet and mobile

• You may be able to save by bundling services together. It could be your internet and mobile plans or even adding energy bills. Check out what's on offer.

• Go paperless as chances are you will be charged extra to be sent a paper bill. You may also be able to get a discount by arranging to pay via direct debit.

• Check your internet speed tier to make sure that it's right for you. You don't want to be paying for NBN 100 if NBN 50 is sufficient. There are a number of handy guides online that can help you work out what you need. Generally, the more people in the house and the more devices you use the higher the speed you'll need. You can always try a slower speed and then move to a faster one if it's not enough. Just check any contract conditions.

• Don't pay for what you don't need. Take a look at how much data you use on average each month. If you are only using 5GB but are paying for 20GB then consider changing plans. Just beware if you go over your data limit you may be charged extra. Consider a plan that slows down your data connection rather than charging extra.

## Streaming

• Make sure you're not paying for what you don't need. Most streaming services offer a number of plans at different prices. If you mostly watch on one device at a time, then opt for the cheaper option which generally only allows you to stream on one screen. And if you mostly stream using your laptop or mobile, you don't really need 4K Ultra HD.

• Subscription hop. There's only so much you can watch at once so there's no need to pay for multiple services each month. Choose one platform, watch everything you want and then cancel it when you're done. You can then sign up for another streaming service and do the same thing. Be sure to make the most of free trials when trying out a new platform.

• Share the costs with family and friends. You pay for one service, your friend pays for another and you just share the access details with each other. Some providers are cracking down on this so it's worth checking the rules.

• Look for bundle deals. Some telco may throw in a streaming service as a freebie or offer a discount if you add the streaming service to your bill. The Optus SubHub platform, for example, lets Optus customers bundle streaming services into one payment. If you add two subscriptions you'll save 5% on each and if you add three or more you'll save 10% on all your subscriptions. Not all streaming services are available on the SubHub platform though.

• Check out free streaming services such as Kanopy and Tubi.

## Car and home insurance

• You may be able to get a discount by bundling. Many insurers will give you discounts if you have more than one policy with them. It's worth finding out how much this could save you.

• Choose a higher excess. The excess is the amount you have to pay if you need to make a claim. Generally the higher the excess the lower the premium. Just make sure that you don't set it too high. You still need to be able to afford to pay it if you need to make a claim.

• Pay annually instead of monthly. The convenience of paying by the month can come at a cost as it is common for insurers to charge more. If you really can't afford to pay for the premium all at once, look for an insurer that doesn't charge extra to pay by the month. Of course, you need to make sure the premiums are still competitive.

• If you don't drive a lot, look into a "pay as you drive" policy. You tell the insurer the number of kilometres you estimate you'll drive in a year and they will calculate your premium based on that. If you end up driving more than you thought, you can let the insurer know and pay to increase the kilometres.

• Limiting the number of drivers listed on your car insurance policy – especially those under 25 – can make your premium cheaper. Just be sure to find out what would happen if someone not listed on your policy drives the car and has an accident. Will you still be covered? In some cases, it will just mean a higher excess.

## Health insurance

• Mix and match – you may find it's cheaper to use one provider for hospital cover and another for extras than getting both through one provider.

• Look at "consciously uncoupling" as there may be no benefit in having a couple policy. Two singles may be cheaper as you're able to remove obstetrics for the male partner while keeping it for the female partner.

• Pay by direct debit. Some insurers may give you a discount if you have the monthly premium direct debited from your account.

• Opt for a higher excess/co-payment. This is the amount you'll have to pay when you use a service. Choosing a higher excess or co-payment can help reduce the premium. You need to be careful with this though because to avoid the Medicare Levy Surcharge you can't have an excess of more than $750 if you're single or more than $1500 if you're part of a couple/family.

• This one requires you to have cash upfront but consider paying your premiums in advance. Health fund fees go up in April each year. Most health funds let you pay a year's health insurance premiums in advance to lock in the previous year's rate.

# YOUR
# MONEY
# MAKEOVER
## STARTS HERE

## WHAT I'VE ACHIEVED SO FAR ...

_____
_____
_____
_____
_____
_____
_____
_____
_____
_____
_____
_____
_____
_____
_____
_____
_____
_____
_____
_____
_____
_____
_____
_____
_____

## TRACK DOWN LOST MONEY & SUPER

There is around $1.5 billion in lost shares, bank accounts and life insurance. To find out if you're entitled to a slice of that pie head to moneysmart.gov.au and type "Find unclaimed money" in the search field. Enter your name to check.

State and territory governments can also be a treasure trove of unclaimed cash. You can find the relevant links at MoneySmart by searching "money held by state governments".

You should also look for any lost super. You'll need a myGov account that is linked to the tax office or you can ask your super fund to search for you. If you have small accounts you may consider consolidating funds. Take a look at Chapter 8 for what to consider before closing any accounts.

_Sell, sell, sell_

**SEARCH YOUR HOUSE FOR 10 THINGS THAT YOU NO LONGER WANT OR NEED. GET THE KIDS TO DO THE SAME – EVEN IF THEY FIND JUST FIVE ITEMS EACH. LIST EVERYTHING FOR SALE ON FACEBOOK MARKETPLACE, GUMTREE OR EBAY.**

## Start the roll the dice challenge

This is one of the fun money-saving challenges I wrote about in Chapter 2. The idea is that you roll a six-sided dice every day and you stash away whatever number it lands on into your savings. If you really want to up the potential savings use two die.

You can get the whole family in on this too – but for younger kids it might be weekly instead of daily.

---

## GIVE YOUR SUPER A HEALTH CHECK

### LOOK AT FOUR KEY AREAS:

### 1. PERFORMANCE: HOW HAS IT PERFORMED OVER THE PAST FIVE YEARS? COMPARE IT WITH FUNDS WITH THE SAME INVESTMENT STRATEGY.

### 2. INVESTMENT OPTION: ARE YOU IN THE RIGHT ONE?

### 3. FEES: HOW MUCH ARE YOU PAYING?

### 4: INSURANCE: WHAT ARE YOU GETTING AND HOW MUCH DOES IT COST?

## GET A COPY OF YOUR CREDIT REPORT & CREDIT SCORE

Check your credit report to make sure there aren't any surprises on it that could affect your chances of getting a loan or could be a warning sign of identity theft.

Your report will include information about any time you have applied for credit, details of any credit accounts you have open or may have had in the past, any defaults and your repayment history on your mortgage or credit card.

You are entitled to check your credit report for free once every three months. You could have a report with more than one agency so it's worth asking each of them for a copy of your report.

The agencies are Equifax (mycreditfile.com.au or 138 332), Experian (experian.com.au or 1300 783 684) and illion (checkyourcredit. com.au or 1300 734 806).

When you get your copy make sure the information is accurate. If you find any mistakes notify the credit reporting agency or the credit provider.

It's also worth checking your credit score. You can do this through sites such as creditsavvy.com.au, creditsimple.com.au, getcreditscore. com.au, wisrcredit.com.au and clearscore.com.au.

# WHAT I'VE ACHIEVED SO FAR ...

........................................

........................................

........................................

........................................

........................................

........................................

........................................

........................................

........................................

........................................

........................................

........................................

........................................

........................................

........................................

........................................

........................................

........................................

........................................

........................................

........................................

........................................

........................................

........................................

........................................

## DITCH A BAD MONEY HABIT

We all have them – a bad habit or two that ends up costing us money. It might be something like always using the dryer instead of hanging out clothes to dry. Canstar crunched the numbers and found that if you put six loads of washing in the dryer each week, it could end up costing you about $330 over a year.

Or maybe you're always forgetting to take a water bottle with you when you are out and about and end up forking out cash to buy a bottle. At about $4 a pop, doing that just once a week will cost you $208 a year.

Mindless spending, not sticking to your list at the supermarket, waiting for your petrol tank to be empty and buying something without comparing prices are other examples.

So, identify one of your bad money habits and make a plan to put an end to it. Use an app like Habit Tracker to record your progress.

## REDUCE CREDIT CARD LIMITS BY 50%

THIS WILL NOT ONLY LOWER THE POTENTIAL DAMAGE YOU CAN DO ON YOUR CARD BUT IT WILL ALSO INCREASE YOUR BORROWING POTENTIAL IF YOU WANT TO APPLY FOR A LOAN AT SOME STAGE IN THE FUTURE.

## Get your will and binding nomination sorted

This is the stuff no one wants to think about – what happens when you die. If you don't have a will, make an appointment with a solicitor to get started on it. If you already have one take another look at it to make sure it reflects your current circumstances. If it doesn't then call your solicitor to set up a time to make the changes.

It's worth noting that your superannuation is not treated like the rest of your estate. It pays to set up a binding death nomination because if you don't the fund's trustees decide who gets your super when you die. Make sure you follow the rules about who you can nominate. Nominations generally need to be reviewed every three years.

## Take your lunch to work

IF YOU'RE BACK IN THE OFFICE AFTER LOCKDOWN TRY NOT TO SLIP INTO THE HABIT OF BUYING YOUR LUNCH. TAKE A PACKED LUNCH AND EACH TIME YOU DO, TRANSFER $15 INTO SAVINGS. BETTER YET, TRANSFER THE MONEY EVEN ON DAYS YOU WORK FROM HOME!

## SUPPORT A CHARITY

CHOOSE A CHARITY AND LOOK FOR WAYS YOU CAN SUPPORT THE CAUSE.

IT COULD BE AS SIMPLE AS MAKING A ONE-OFF DONATION, SETTING UP A REGULAR CONTRIBUTION OR EXPLORING VOLUNTEER OPTIONS.

YOU MAY ALSO CONSIDER GETTING A FEW FRIENDS TOGETHER AND HOSTING AN EVENT TO RAISE FUNDS OR USING A PLATFORM SUCH AS GOFUNDME OR MYCAUSE TO FUNDRAISE.

## WHAT I'VE ACHIEVED SO FAR ...

........................................................
........................................................
........................................................
........................................................
........................................................
........................................................
........................................................
........................................................
........................................................
........................................................
........................................................
........................................................
........................................................
........................................................
........................................................
........................................................
........................................................
........................................................
........................................................
........................................................
........................................................
........................................................

## TOP UP YOUR SUPER

ADDING EVEN A SMALL AMOUNT OF MONEY TO YOUR SUPER CAN MAKE A BIG DIFFERENCE IN THE FUTURE – YOU MIGHT BE SURPRISED BY JUST HOW MUCH.

LET'S SAY, FOR EXAMPLE, YOU'RE 24 YEARS OLD AND YOU GIVE UP ONE $20 BOTTLE OF WINE PER WEEK AND INSTEAD POP THAT INTO YOUR SUPER. ASSUMING 5.2% GROWTH, YOU'LL ENJOY AN EXTRA $54,000 IN YOUR SUPER FUND WHEN YOU RETIRE.

CONSIDER SETTING UP A REGULAR SALARY SACRIFICE CONTRIBUTION.

## SET UP A FISCAL DATE NIGHT AND A FAMILY MONEY LUNCH

The only way to make sure everyone is on the same page when it comes to financial goals is to talk!

If you have a partner, arrange a date night to chat money. Check out Chapter 6 for ideas on topics but it's all about coming up with a plan you can work towards.

If you're part of a family with kids then that's another session. Chat about what everyone would like to achieve and what you can all do to get there. If everyone is involved then they will feel more accountable.

## Time to splurge

ARRANGE DINNER AT A RESTAURANT YOU WOULDN'T NORMALLY GO TO OR BOOK GOLD CLASS MOVIE TICKETS FOR THE FAMILY – THE SPLURGE OPTIONS ARE ENDLESS. SOMETIMES IT'S NICE TO TREAT YOURSELF AFTER WORKING SO HARD.

## Do a subscription audit

Netflix, Stan, Foxtel, Audible, Spotify, HelloFresh, your gym membership ... these monthly subscriptions can really add up.

Make a list of all your subscriptions and think hard about whether you really need them all.

Ditch any subscriptions you are no longer getting any real value from. You can potentially save a decent chunk of cash.

If you really miss them you can always subscribe again.

## HAVE A MEAL PREP DAY

One of the reasons a lot of us resort to picking up a takeaway meal on the way home from work or ordering delivery from the comfort of our couch is that we just can't be bothered cooking.

Having a selection of readymade meals waiting for you in the freezer means you don't have to spend money on takeaway on those nights when you're just too tired.

So today, head to the supermarket and buy everything you need to cook a few meals that you can freeze. Bolognese, curries and soups are ideal for this.

## DELETE AN APP THAT IS COSTING YOU MONEY

CONVENIENCE APPS SUCH AS UBER, UBER EATS, MENULOG AND AFTERPAY CAN COME AT A COST. THEY MAKE IT JUST TOO EASY FOR US TO SPEND.

SO DITCH ONE APP THAT YOU FEEL MAKES YOU SPEND AND REPLACE IT WITH ONE THAT CAN HELP YOU SAVE OR MAKE MONEY!

# WHAT I'VE ACHIEVED SO FAR ...

## CREATE A 'WHEN I DIE' FILE FOR YOUR FAMILY

It may feel a bit morbid – and I hope the day is a long while away – but having all your important information in one place will make your loved ones lives so much easier when thar day comes. Here are some of the things to include:

• Your will and binding nomination.

• Documents such as your birth certificate, marriage or divorce certificate and passport.

• Bank account details including passwords for online banking.

• Super account details and documents relating to other investments.

• Details of your life insurance policy.

• Passwords for your computer, social media accounts, phone etc.

• Contact details for your lawyer and accountant.

• Any special funeral instructions.

## CALCULATE YOUR RETIREMENT NUMBER

THERE ARE THREE FACTORS TO CONSIDER WHEN WORKING OUT THIS NUMBER – THE ANNUAL COST OF YOUR DREAM RETIREMENT LIFESTYLE, WHEN YOU WANT TO RETIRE AND YOUR LIFE EXPECTANCY. YOU'LL FIND MORE INFO IN CHAPTER 16.

## Find a better place to stash your cash

No one should really be paying any fees on their everyday account and if you are it is definitely time to switch!

Look for ways you could be getting extra value from your transaction account such as cashback, foreign ATM rebates or no foreign currency conversion fees when you shop online from overseas sites or when you travel internationally.

Also check if you could get a higher interest rate for your savings. There are often promotional rates that could be worth switching for. Just make sure you look at what the rate reverts to when the introductory offer ends.

## Boost your savings

**INCREASE THE AMOUNT YOU ARE DIRECTING TO YOUR SAVINGS BY AT LEAST 5%.**

**SO IF YOU'RE SAVING $100 A WEEK, UP THAT TO $105 OR IF YOU'RE SAVING $300 INCREASE IT TO $315.**

**IF YOU'RE SAVING ZILCH THOUGH AIM HIGHER THAN 5%, START BY SAVING 10% OF YOUR TAKE-HOME PAY.**

## SIGN UP TO A CASHBACK SERVICE

**CASHBACK SITES AND APPS GIVE YOU A SHARE OF THE COMMISSION THEY GET FROM RETAILERS WHEN YOU SHOP THROUGH THEIR PLATFORM. SO YOU GET CASH BACK AFTER YOU MAKE A PURCHASE.**

**CHECK OUT CASHREWARDS, SHOPBACK, KICKBACK AND CASHBACK CLUB. SUPER REWARDS AND BOOST YOUR SUPER ARE SIMILAR BUT THE CASH GOES TO YOUR SUPER.**

# WHAT I'VE ACHIEVED SO FAR ...

_Buy nothing new for one week_

RESIST THE URGE TO SPLURGE FOR JUST SEVEN DAYS. SURE, YOU'RE ALLOWED TO BUY GROCERIES BUT NO NEW SHOES OR CLOTHES! YOUR WALLET WILL THANK YOU.

## START INVESTING

The thought of investing – and potentially losing – your hard-earned money can be scary for some. Don't be consumed by investor paralysis and do nothing. Get out of your comfort zone and invest – even if it's $1000.

As for where to invest, don't over-complicate things. There really are only a handful of options you can invest in – yourself, cash, fixed income, property and equities. To get a better understanding of various options check out Chapter 7.

Then choose an ETF, buy a parcel of shares or you can even invest your small change in ETFs through micro investing platforms like Raiz. Note that fees hit small balances hard so be sure to beef up your balance.

Making money is about buying good-quality assets and holding them for a reasonable time.

## TRACK YOUR SPENDING

**I'M NOT TALKING ABOUT THE BIG THINGS BUT THE INCIDENTALS – YOUR MORNING LATTE, THE MASCARA YOU BOUGHT ON YOUR LUNCH BREAK, THE APP YOU DOWNLOADED. JUST FOR ONE WEEK JOT DOWN EVERY LITTLE PURCHASE YOU MAKE. IT MIGHT BE QUITE EYE OPENING TO SEE WHERE YOUR MONEY IS GOING.**

## LOOK AT YOUR LIFE & INCOME PROTECTION

When was the last time you looked at your life insurance? Do you have any, not enough or maybe too much?

Ideally the amount should be enough to pay out any debt such as the mortgage, cover funeral costs and ensure the family has sufficient ongoing cash flow.

You should also make sure you have adequate income protection insurance, which generally covers you for a maximum of 75% of your salary, if you can't work due to sickness, accident or injury.

You'll also need to decide whether to take cover inside or outside super. It can be complex and worth getting professional advice on what's best.

---

*Find out if you're entitled to any government payments*

The federal government offers a range of payments to Aussies to help with the costs of raising kids, your health and to support those looking for work, for example.

Take a look at the Services Australia website (servicesaustralia.gov. au) to get an idea of the payments that may be available. Search for the "Payment and service finder" tool which can also be helpful. You are asked a series of questions and it will show you the payments you might be eligible for and estimate the amount. You will need to formally apply for any payments.

State and territory governments also have various payments available. It's worth looking into what's on offer in your area.

# Acknowledgements

Behind every successful, hard-working woman is another woman who's just as good (and has your back!). I'd like to thank Maria Bekiaris for her hard work, ideas, input and guidance not only on this book but also as my sounding board in life. We truly have a wonderful partnership. We both have daughters and hope that this book – our gift to them – helps Nicky and Liv go on to become financially independent young women.

A big thank you to Nicola Field, who also assisted with the research (this woman fears no deadlines), and Phil Slade, for his behavioural insights into why we do what we do (see Chapter 14). They were invaluable.

Thank you also to Sally Eagle, who was my publisher for the first edition of this book, and the inspiration behind a few of these chapters. She had been hounding me for some time to write something but it was only when she waltzed into my office one afternoon in one of her amazing ensembles, pregnant with her fourth child and wondering how the hell she was going to juggle everything, did it click with me that there was a need for a girl's guide to money.

And last but not least, a big thank you to Paul Clitheroe, the original money guru and one of Australia's most respected finance experts, who 20-odd years ago saw behind the pigtails and gave me a job that I still absolutely cherish. His personal saving tip about occasionally forgetting to bring your wallet to lunch – he was known to do that back when we were filming the popular Channel 9 program *Money* in the late 1990s – has also worked well for me.